SAUDI ARABIA PRIVACY LAW

Michael O'Kane

ISBN (Print): 978-1-945979-15-6
ISBN (E-Book): 978-1-945979-18-7

ANDULUS
PUBLISHING

CHAPTER ONE

Introduction

In the global march to recover privacy, cybersecurity has become a matter of the highest priority. Very public data breaches and cyberattacks have become routine. Companies have been forced to shut down while negotiating with cyberterrorists. Adobe, Facebook and other reputable companies have seen the privacy walls breached and their customer lists published on the Internet. Sony Pictures saw the publication of embarrassing intra-company emails and the leak of unreleased movies. In view of these and other criminal acts, legislators reached the obvious conclusion that both the private sector and government had failed in their obligation to protect personal data and something needed to be done.

Rules regarding privacy have long been in flux. A right to privacy was recognized at least by the end of the 19th century, but a century later the widespread use of social media and the sharing ethos of the Internet made public what was once private. Some believe that the privacy genie has long escaped his bottle and those who complain about the loss of privacy are crybaby Luddites afraid of the Internet's brave new world. Others claim that it is not too late to put the genie back into his bottle and have enacted legislation to do so We are only now beginning to see whether these efforts will be successful.

In some countries, efforts to bring back and reinforce privacy have failed. The United States has no general legislation on the topic. The idea of a "right to privacy" was recognized in the United

States as early as 1888, and shortly thereafter was written about in an influential article by Louis Brandeis, later Chief Justice of New York's highest court. But by the mid-20th century, despite the work of various State legislatures, American courts failed to enforce privacy rights. By turning to the common law principle of "standing," that is, showing actual harm, US courts made the enforcement of privacy rights difficult. (5). "Standing," is based on the idea that there is no constitutional "case or controversy" unless a plaintiff has suffered an injury. Since federal courts are courts of limited jurisdiction, there is no place for philosophical, conjectural or hypothetical injuries. In short, no injury, no case.

Data breaches happen every day. On February 11, a breach involving a US State government agency was announced, affecting 650,000 license holders and containing names, national identifying numbers and other personal information.[1]

With respect to the disclosure of sensitive personal information, In *Rudgayzer v. Yahoo! Inc.*,[2] the court held that "[m]ere disclosure" of personal information "without a showing of actual harm" is "insufficient to support a claim of breach of contract." In *In re Facebook Privacy Litigation*, the court rejected plaintiffs' theory they suffered "appreciable and actual damage" in a suit for breach of contract."[3] Ibid. at p. 60.

Even when there is a clear violation of disclosure rules, there is no judicial remedy. *Senne v. Village of Palatine*, 784 F.3d.444 (7th Cir. 2015).

This does not mean that the high tech majors are unregulated. In 2019, the US Federal Trade Commission imposed a $5 billion fine against Facebook for violating a 2012 FTC order by "deceiving" its customers concerning their ability to control their personal

---

[1] https://www.king5.com/article/news/local/washington-licensing-data-breach-cyber/281-58c15b24-b4b6-4e77-b975-a1d232042943

[2] *Rudgayzer v. Yahoo! Inc.*, 5:12-CV-01399 EJD, 2012 WL 5471149 (N.D. Cal. Nov. 9, 2012), appeal dismissed (Dec. 13, 2012)

[3] Cited in "Privacy Harms" Citron & Solove, 102 B.U.L.-(2022) at p.59,60; found at SSRN-id3782222.pdf; https://papers.ssrn.com/sol3/papers.cfm?abstract_id=3782222

information.[4]

In the absence of a general federal statute States have enacted their own legislation. New York requires financial firms to appoint a chief information security officer, implement a cybersecurity program, perform risk assessments and report breaches within 72 hours.[5]

The field has been left to the country's fifty squabbling States. The European Union has taken the lead in privacy legislation, enacting the General Data Protection Regulation (GDPR)[6] in 2016. This law imposes strict penalties on companies that fail to safeguard personal data in their possession. Companies that ignore the GDPR do so at their peril. Google was just fined by a court in Germany for failing to meet the high standards of the GDPR. The Austrian data regulator decided that European citizen personal data could not be transferred to the United States since there the data would not be protected.

In February, 2022, Yahoo! Japan announced that it was closing down its operations in the European Union because of the high cost of complying with European regulations, presumably including the GDPR.[7]

Saudi Arabia has responded to all these events by enacting various laws and creating new agencies to administer them. It is in this environment that the country decided to follow the European example.

Saudi Arabia's constitution[8] provides that

"[t]elegraphic, postal, telephone, and other means of communications shall be safeguarded. They cannot be confiscated,

---

[4] https://www.ftc.gov/news-events/press-releases/2019/07/ftc-imposes-5-billion-penalty-sweeping-new-privacy-restrictions

[5] *Privacy, Regulations and Cybersecurity: The Essential Business Guide,* Chris Moschovitis Wiley, 2021 (hereinafter "Moschovitis") at p. 323

[6] Regulation (EU) 2016/679. The law became effective in all EU countries in May, 2018.

[7] "Yahoo! Japan is Going Dark in Europe," https://www.theverge.com/2022/2/1/22911965/yahoo-japan-europe-offline-regulations-compliance-gdpr

[8] Called the Basic Law of Governance (1992).

delayed, read or listened to except as provided by law."[9]

It is upon this foundation that the country's data privacy laws are constructed.

---

[9] Basic Law, Art. 40.

CHAPTER TWO

SDAIA

Prior to September, 2021, Saudi Arabia had no national law to protect private personal information. This changed with the passage of the Personal Data Protection Law[10] (the "Law").

The Law assigns oversight authority to the Saudi Data and Artificial Intelligence Authority ("SDAIA"), a new Saudi agency. A two-year transitional period has been established during which jurisdiction over these matters is to be transferred to this agency, with some exceptions. This is important because previously the Saudi agency with authority over these matters was the Communications and Information Technology Commission ("CITC"). The CITC has a policy of requiring servers containing personal data to be located in Saudi Arabia. It is not clear whether the SDAIA will carry this policy forward as jurisdiction is transferred and in accordance with forthcoming implementing regulations overseen by the SDAIA.

Entities that collect private information are defined as "controllers."[11] The term refers to entities which collect personal information for the purpose of processing it. Restrictions are placed

---

[10] Royal Decree M/19 of 9/2/1443H (16 September 2021), approving Council of Minsters Resolution No. 98 dated 7/2/1443H (14 September 2021). References are to articles of this law.

[11] Article 1(18).

on controllers concerning what they may do with personal data collected,[12] and includes data relating to Kingdom residents by a party outside the Kingdom.[13] This is significant because the provision recognizes that such processing takes place, despite the broad prohibition contained in Article 18 of the Law.

Financial data is considered "sensitive" under the Law.[14] The processing of personal data collected by a controller requires the written consent of the individual from whom the data is collected.[15] Consent is not required where it is in implementation of an existing agreement to which the person is a party.[16]

The controller may not require consent as a condition of accessing the service. Specifically, consent may not be "a condition for the provision of a service,"[17] unless the service sought is data processing itself. Consent is key because a controller may only collect data from the individual or a "publicly available source."[18] Public available sources of information in Saudi Arabia are few.

Consent is not required when personal data is to be used for the purposes of scientific, research or statistical purposes.[19]

The Personal Data Protection Law

The Personal Data Protection Law "PDPL")[20], enacted on September 16, 2021, is Saudi Arabia's dramatic response to the

---

[12] Article 2.

[13] Article 2(1). The Law does not apply to personal or family use, making use of applications such as Facebook permissible. Article 2(2).

[14] Article 11. The context in this article is information related to credit applications and credit history. We think the category is wide enough to encompass all types of personal financial information.

[15] Article 5.

[16] Article 6(2). This paragraph is in the nature of a grandfather clause insofar as it does not seek to impose the Law on existing agreements. It is again unclear whether this is a general exception to the Article 18 prohibition on transborder data transfers or whether that prohibition adds a new condition to existing contracts.

[17] Article 10.

[18] Article 10.

[19] Article 27.

[20] Royal Decree No. M/19, dated 9/2/1443 (16 Sep. 2021) The law takes effect on March 23, 2022.

erosion of personal privacy in the age of the Internet, in a country that has prized personal privacy as a feature of its unique culture.

The Law assigns responsibility for policing the use of individual data and data processing to a new agency, the Saudi Data and Artificial Intelligence Authority ("SDAIA"). The new agency's name bespeaks its cutting-edge nature; while the long negotiations concerning the Law were taking place, the decision as to which agency would be assigned these duties was controversial. In the end, a new agency was given the responsibility.

The most dramatic provision of the law prohibits the transmission of Saudi personal data outside the Kingdom without permission or license except in extreme circumstances.[21] Given that transborder data transfer is commonplace today, those who engage routinely in the practice have voiced justifiable alarm, pointing out that they will have to significantly revise their business practices or stop doing business in the Kingdom altogether.

There are perhaps two approaches: on the one hand, SDAIA could issue blanket licenses to data controllers permitting the routine transfer of data in their possession. In that case, the PDPL would be a mere set of guidelines warning against bad behavior. On the other hand, the Law may very well be a red line which may not be crossed. A relaxed attitude towards the most profound invasions of self possible is no longer appropriate and those who think otherwise are advised to modify their conduct.

In addition to the PDPL, another law requires that government agencies improve their data security. Royal Decree number 57231, dated 10/11/1439 H, states that "all government organizations must improve their cybersecurity level to protect their networks, systems and data, and comply with NCA's policies, framework, standards, controls and guidelines."

It remains to be seen which of these approaches will be taken. Consultations with stakeholder agencies are in progress, with implementing regulations promised around the time the law will take effect.

Personal Data Protection Law Summary

The PDPL defines both "personal" and "sensitive" data. Personal data is any information which may lead to the identification of an

---

[21] Art. 29, PDPL.

individual.[22] "Sensitive" data is that which concerns the status of that individual, such as "ethnic or tribal origin, religious, intellectual or political belief, or indicates his membership in associations or civil institutions, as well as criminal and security data, biometric identification data, genetic data, credit data or health data, location data and data that indicates that the individual is of unknown parentage."[23]

Owners[24] (called "Data Subjects") have the right to know what their data is being used for, have the right to a copy of the data at no charge (subject to credit reporting rules) and have right to correct or delete erroneous data.[25]

Those who receive personal information are deemed "data controllers" and new obligations are imposed on them under the PDPL. Owner consent to collection is required[26], with few exceptions:

- if the processing is for the owner and contacting him is difficult.
- when the processing is in accordance with another law or in implementation of a previous agreement to which the owner is a party; or
- if the data controller is a public company.[27]

Consent to collection may not be a condition of providing services,

---

[22] The CITC's definition is "Any information, regardless of its source or form, which would lead to identifying the customer, or that would render the customer identifiable directly or indirectly, including, but not limited to, names, ID numbers, addresses, contact numbers, licenses and registrations numbers and personal properties, bank account numbers and credit cards numbers, customer's photos or videos, as well as any other data of personal nature." Resolution 415.

[23] Article 1, PDPL. Draft implementing regulations address military and national security subjects, but for convenience we omit these in our discussion here.

[24] However, the term "owner" will be used herein.

[25] Art. 4, PDPL.

[26] Art. 5, PDPL. Collection for scientific or research purposes does not require consent where the information does not identify a particular individual. Art. 27 PDPL

[27] Art. 6, PDPL.

unless those services include data processing itself.[28] Personal data may only be held for a limited period[29] and must be collected from the Owner himself[30] and for a proper purpose.[31]

The Law sets forth where disclosure to third-parties is permitted and when it is not.[32] Disclosure is not permitted in the following cases:

- threat to security
- diplomatic relations threatened
- impedes law enforcement
- endangers individual safety
- violates third-party privacy
- conflicts with interests of a ward
- breaches professional obligation
- involves a breach of an obligation
- discloses a confidential source

Disclosure is permitted where:

- the Owner agrees
- the data is collected from a public source
- for security reasons
- to protect public safety

as long as identifying personal information is deleted.

SDAIA is to be notified in case of leaks[33] and in no case less than 72 hours following discovery of any breach. Advertising sent without consent or an "easy unsubscribe" is prohibited.[34]

SDAIA requires the registration of, and asserts jurisdiction over, data controllers.[35] Because of the broad definition of personal information and the fact every company requires the provision of that personal information to SDAIA, in theory every single company in the Kingdom would be required to register and pay a

---

[28] Art. 7, PDPL.

[29] Art. 9, PDPL.

[30] Art. 10, PDPL.

[31] Art. 11, PDPL.

[32] Art. 15, 16, PDPL.

[33] Art. 20, PDPL

[34] Art. 25, PDPL. Marketing with consent is permitted. Art. 26.

[35] Articles 30-33,PDPL

fee of up to SAR 100,000.[36]This provision requires clarification and hopefully guidance will be covered by the forthcoming regulations.

Each organization subject to the law must establish a unit in charge of developing, documenting and monitoring implementation of the PDPL.

In all cases except where there is an official request, consent of the data provider is required.

The PDPL's Article 29 generally prohibits transborder data transfer where the data involves Saudi residents. Data may not be transferred outside Kingdom except in cases of extreme necessity or to prevent or treat infection. There are few exceptions, such as where there is a treaty requirement, or where a decision has been made that export is in the interest of the Kingdom, where national security is not prejudiced, where sufficient guarantees are provided and the amount of data exported is limited to that amount necessary to meet the stated goals.

Approval by SDAIA is required. SDAIA may make exceptions on a case by case basis where controller provides guarantees.[37]It is not clear whether SDAIA will grant blanket authorizations to entities such as banks. Consultations with SAMA and other Saudi agencies are continuing concerning this and other matters to be covered in the Implementing Regulations before the Law takes effect.

Penalties for Violation of the PDPL

PDPL compliance and implementation are not optional, they are a requirement. The Law imposes both criminal and civil penalties. Non-compliance with the Law is subject to administrative action. Unauthorized disclosure or transborder data transfer are the only two specified crimes.[38] Other violations of the Law are not deemed criminal.[39] This highlights the importance SDAIA gives to transborder data transfers. Criminal penalties are always serious.

Criminal penalties for violating the provisions of the PDPL are as

---

[36] Art. 32, PDPL.
[37] Art. 29, PDPL.
[38] Art. 35, PDPL.
[39] Art. 36, PDPL.

follows:

1. Unauthorized disclosure of personal data: 2 years' imprisonment and a SAR 3 million fine
2. Unauthorized offshore transfer: 1 years' imprisonment or SAR 1 million fine
3. Any other violation: warning or a SAR 5 million fine.

Recidivism doubles penalties.

CHAPTER THREE

Classification of Information

The National Data Management Office set forth rules requiring government agencies to classify the data in their possession.[40] The rules only apply to Saudi government agencies[41] and for that reason may have escaped notice by the private sector. These classification rules are nevertheless useful guidelines for determining the sensitivity of data held by the private sector. They must in any case be followed in the context of data shared while executing government contracts, even by subcontractors who have no direct contractual relationship with a government entity.

The Regulations require data to be classified based on its potential adverse impact were it to be improperly or inadvertently disclosed[42] and establishes key principles:

Principle 1:

"Data should be accessible (in development sectors) unless its nature or sensitivity requires a higher level of classification and protection; and top secret (in the political and security sectors) unless its nature or sensitivity requires a lower level of classification and protection.

---

[40] Issued by the National Data Management Office June 1, 2020 v 1.0

[41] §4.1 refers to "public entities."

[42] §4.2

Principle 2: Classification Based on Necessity

Where data must be classified, the level of classification, and the safeguards and controls associated with the classification level, should be based on the potential adverse impact as a result of unauthorized disclosure, subject to the nature and sensitivity of the data.

Principle 3: Timely Classification

Data should be classified upon creation or upon being received from another entity and the classification exercise should be time bound.

Principle 4: Highest Level of Protection

If information includes an integrated set of data with different classification levels, the highest classification level should be applied to the aggregated data.

Principle 5: Segregation of Duties

Duties of participants in the classification process should not overlap in terms of classifying data, approving a classification decision, granting authorization for access or usage of data, accessing data, protecting data, or disposal of data – in a way that does not lead to overlapping specialization or dissipation of liability.

Principle 6: Need to Know

Access to data should be provided only if there is legitimate requirement for usage of the data based on authorization and access controls and for the least number of people possible.

Principle 7: Least Privilege

Access to and use of data should be limited to the minimal access required to satisfy the needs of the assigned. "

The classification work flow is shown in the following chart:

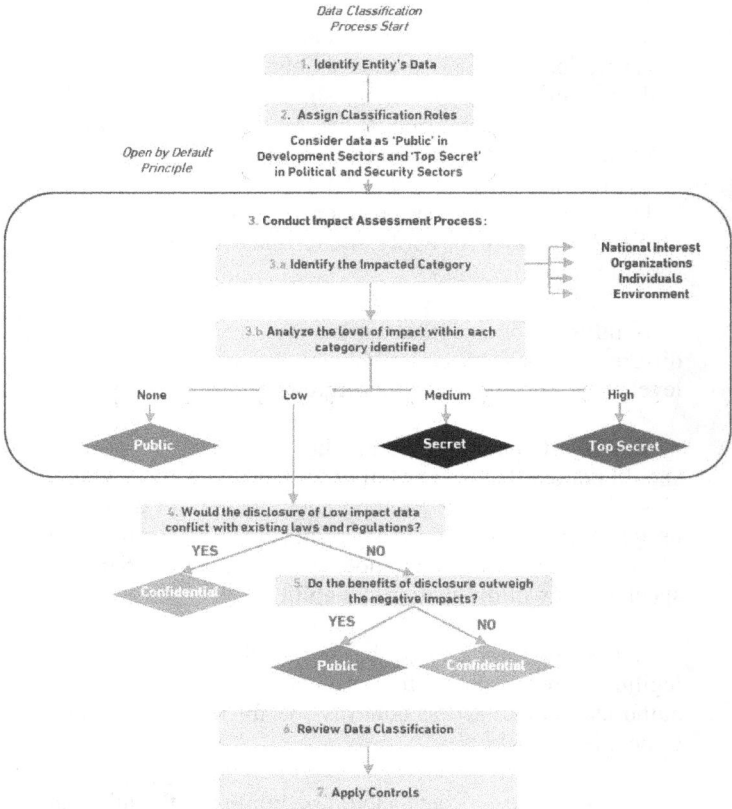

(Graphic from NDMO)

Classification Levels

- Top Secret
- Secret
- Confidential[43]
- Public

---

[43] Interestingly, the USG has another level between Confidential and Public, FOUO, ("for official use only.")

CHAPTER FOUR

Personal Data Protection Standards

The National Data Management Office issued rules entitled, *Data Management and Personal Data Protection Standards* in August, 2020 and has regularly updated the guidance since. The latest issue is version 1.5, dated June, 2021. The *Standards* rely on guidance issued by the Data Management International Association (DAMA), a multinational study group active in 33 countries.

The *Standards* provide a comprehensive set of rules governing data protection in the Kingdom. They predate and so are in addition to, the more specific rules found in the PDPL. The *Standards* apply to government agencies and "business partners handling government data." Unlike the more limited jurisdiction over the private sector only when it comes to sensitive national infrastructure under the jurisdiction of the NCA, this application of the *Standards* is much more expansive. Any company performing a government contract will "handle government data." Additionally, any company that seeks the award of a government contract or has performed work as a prime or subcontractor on any kind of government or government funded contract is covered under the *Standards.*

"Government data" for these purposes includes:

[All] data regardless of form or type including paper records, emails, data stored in electronic form, voice recordings, videos, maps, photos, scripts, handwritten documents, or any other form of recorded data.

An annual compliance audit is required. Such audit is to be submitted to the NDMO in the third quarter of each year. The agency's (or in the case of included private sector entities) Chief Data Officer will be in charge of the audit.

Data processing systems must be implemented proactively so as to protect the privacy of individuals encompassing the requirements of consent, refusal and withdrawal.

In a major change from past practice, the *Standards* enshrine the principle that Saudi government data is public by default unless there is a "sufficient justification" that non-disclosure is in the public interest. The same same principle was established at the time of the enactment in the United States of the Freedom of Information Act, but no sooner was the law passed that government agencies ferociously fought disclosure by expanding the exceptions to the law, delaying disclosure for years, complaining that no funds had been appropriated for disclosure reviews, forcing requesters to pay exorbitant fees and other means of evading the clear intent of the law. The Saudi government has historically been secretive, consistent with national culture. Whether easy and efficient access to government data will henceforth be the rule remains to be seen.

The *Standards* include a structure for personal data protection, defined as "focus[ing] on [the] protection of a subject's entitlement to the proper handling and non-disclosure of their personal information. Personal data protections are afforded the highest priority under the *Standards*.

Each agency must establish an implementation strategy which contains a Personal Data Protection Plan with a three-year implementation deadline. Each agency must establish a data management office, led by a Chief Data Officer, to coordinate implementation of the strategy. A legal advisor must also be appointed. As there is no stated requirement that these functions be performed in-house, in the absence of other guidance they may be outsourced.

The *Standards* require agencies to publish the contact details of those persons to whom a valid license has been issued, including the following *sensitive* information:

* * *

1. Names
2. Postal addresses
3. E-mail addresses

(FOI3.3, p. 145, *Standards*)

There is obviously conflict between protecting private information pertaining to individual licensees and the public's right to know that an individual is qualified and holds an appropriate license.

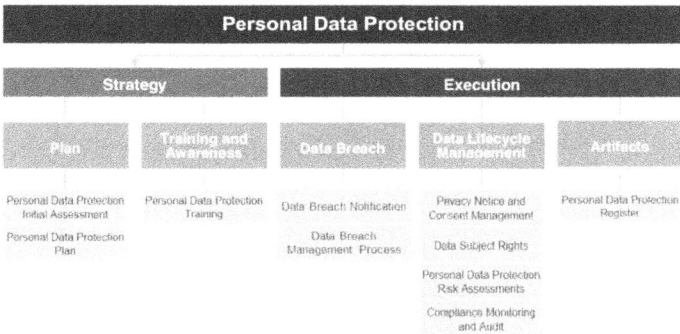

The agency must perform a personal data assessment which is to include the:

1. Identification of types of personal data being collected
2. Location and method of storage of personal data
3. Current processing and uses of the personal data
4. Privacy challenges to meet compliance with the National Data Management Office's Personal Data Protection Regulations.

Each agency shall also conduct a training program to highlight to employees the importance of protecting personal data. Procedures for requesting consent of the subject for the collection, use or disclosure of personal information must be implemented if they are not already in place. A privacy notice must be provided. Data rights management must include the following protections:

1. Right to be informed
2. Right to access
3. Right to rectification
4. Right to erasure
5. Right to object
6. Right to restrict processing
7. Right to data portability

Note that these protections are consistently with those found in the GDPR. The NDMO references both the GDPR and the California Consumer Privacy Act as sources for these guidelines.

Annual audits are required and any data breach must be reported within 72 hours.

CHAPTER FIVE

Personal Data Interim Regulations

In 2020, the Saudi Arabia's National Data Management Office issued Personal Data Interim Regulations (PDIR) as part of its National Data Governance Interim Regulations.

Scope

The PDIR applies to "all entities in the Kingdom that process personal data…[and] all entities outside the Kingdom that process personal data related to individuals residing in the Kingdom."[44] What is an entity? "Public entity" is a defined term, a government agency. "Entity" itself is not defined.

Is the word 'public' missing? If so, would apply only to government agencies. Given the stated scope, would not apply to private entities. However, there are good reasons to believe that similar restrictions will eventually be imposed on the private sector

The PDIR also includes online data processing.

* * *

---

[44] §5.1

Key Principles:[45]

"Principle 1: Accountability

Data Controller's privacy policies and procedures shall be identified, documented and approved by the head of entity (or his designee) and circulated to all concerned parties.

Principle 2: Transparency

A notice of Data Controller's privacy policies and procedures – Privacy Notice – shall be drawn up indicating the purposes for which personal data will be collected in a clear, easy to understand language.

Principle 3: Choice and Consent

The purpose for collection of any personally identifying data shall be shall be made clear to Data Subject and their (implicit / explicit) approval shall be obtained regarding collection, use and/or disclosure of personal data before collection.

Principle 4: Limiting Data Collection

Collection of any personal data shall be limited to minimum data that enables fulfillment of purposes provided for in Privacy Notice.

Principle 5: Use, Retention and Destruction

Personal data usage shall be restricted to purposes provided for in Privacy Notice, which the Data Subject has implicitly or explicitly approved. Moreover, Data shall be retained as long as necessary to achieve their intended purposes or as required by laws and regulations. Furthermore, data shall be destroyed it in a safe manner that prevents leakage, loss, theft, misuse or unauthorized access.

Principle 6: Access to Data

---

[45] §5.2

Entities shall provide a means by which any Data Subject can review, update and correct their personal data.

Principle 7: Data Disclosure Limitation

Disclosure of personal data to third parties shall be restricted to the purposes provided for in Privacy Notice, which was approved by Data Subject.

Principle 8: Data Security

Personal data shall be protected from leakage, damage, loss, theft, misuse, modification, or unauthorized access – according to the controls issued by the National Cybersecurity Authority and the relevant authorities.

Principle 9: Data Quality

Personal data shall be maintained after verification of its accuracy, completeness and timeliness, and such data shall be directly relevant to purposes provided for in Privacy Notice.

Principle 10: Monitoring and Compliance

Compliance with Data Controller's privacy policies and procedures shall be monitored, and any privacy-related inquires, complaints, and disputes shall be addressed."

Data Subject Rights[46]

The PDIR establishes rights held by those from whom data is collected:

First: The right to be informed of the Legal Basis and the purpose concerning the collection and processing of their personal information. Personal Data may not be collected or processed without Data Subject,,s express consent and all processing must be consistent with the agreed upon Legal Basis.

Second: The right to withdraw his consent – at any time – unless statutory or judicial requirements require

---

[46] §5.3

otherwise.

Third: The right to access his personal data within the possession of the Data Controller, including access to, request to correct, complete or update personal data, and request to destroy unnecessary data, and get a copy of such data in a clear format.[47]

Data controllers are responsible for the development of each entities' privacy policy and procedures.[48] Approval by the entity's chief officer is required. §5.4(2) also contemplates the creation of an independent agency to monitor the development and implementation of privacy policies and procedures. Presumably, this agency is SDAIA.

The PDIR impose obligations on the entity's data controller. These are as follows:

- "The Data Controller shall be accountable for development and enforcement of policies and procedures in respect of personal data protection. The head of entity (or his designee) shall be accountable for approval of such policies and procedures.

- The Data Controller shall review and update Service Level Contracts and Agreements in accordance with privacy policies and procedures adopted by Controller's senior management/governance committee.

- The Data Controller shall launch awareness programs to promote and raise awareness of privacy culture in accordance with privacy policies and procedures adopted by the Controller's senior management/governance committee.

- The Data Subject shall be notified of other sources that are used in case all data are indirectly collected (from other parties).

- The Data Subject,,s approval shall be obtained for personal data collection, processing and sharing after determining the approval type (explicit or implicit) based on the data nature and collection methods.

- Data content shall be limited to the minimum data required

---

[47] §5.3
[48] §5.4

for achieving the purpose of collection.
- Data shall be used only for the purpose for which it is collected.
- The Data Controller shall store and process the personal data within the Kingdom's territory in order to ensure preservation of the digital national sovereignty over such data. These personal data may only be processed outside the Kingdom after the Controller obtains a written approval from the Regulatory Authority and the Regulatory Authority shall coordinate with NDMO."

Furthermore,
- "The Data Controller shall prepare and document data erasure procedures and policies in order to destroy the data in a secure manner, that prevents data loss, misuse or unauthorized access – including operational and archived data and backups – according to controls issued by the National Cybersecurity Authority.
- The Data Controller shall include data retention and destruction policy provisions in any agreements to be concluded with other Data Processors.
- The Data Controller shall determine the means through which the Data Subject can access his personal data for the purpose of data review and updating.
- The Data Controller shall verify Data Subject's identity before granting him access to his personal data according to the controls approved by the National Cybersecurity Authority and the relevant authorities.
- Personal data shall not be shared with any other entities except for the purposes specified subject to the Data Subject's approval and according to the laws and regulations; provided that these other entities are provided with the relevant privacy procedures and policies and such procedures and policies are included in the contracts and agreements concluded therewith. The Data Subject shall be notified, and his approval shall be obtained if his data are to be shared with other entities to be used in other purposes.
- The Data Controller shall obtain NDMO's approval – having coordinated with the Regulatory Authority – prior

to sharing the personal data with other entities outside the Kingdom.

- The Data Controller shall develop and document the steps necessary for ensuring that the personal data are accurate, integral, updated and used for the purpose for which they are collected. The administrative guidelines and technical measures adopted by the Controller for information security shall be followed in order to ensure personal data protection, including but not limited to:

Grant data access privileges in accordance with employees duties and responsibilities.

Apply the administrative procedures and technical measures that document data processing stages and allow identifying the user responsible for each stage (processing records).

- Employees who are initiating data processing operations sign a nondisclosure and confidentiality undertaking to only disclose such data in accordance with the policies, procedures, laws and regulations. o For data processing, the honest and responsible employees shall be assigned according to data nature and sensitivity and access policy approved by the Controller."

And additionally,

- "Use the appropriate security measures (For example: Encryption, and separate the environments relating to development) in order to protect personal data in accordance with data nature and sensitivity and means used to transfer and store data according to controls approved by the National Cybersecurity Authority and the relevant authorities.

- The Data Controller should periodically monitor compliance with privacy procedures and policies and present the same to the head of the entity (or his designee). The corrective procedures to be taken should be determined in case of non-compliance and the Regulatory Authority and NDMO should be notified according to the reporting lines. "

* * *

Export of Data

Both the PDPL and §5.4 of the PDIR require that personal data relating to Saudi citizens not be exported:

The Data Controller shall store and process the personal data within the Kingdom's territory in order to ensure preservation of the digital national sovereignty over such data. These personal data may only be processed outside the Kingdom after the Controller obtains a written approval from the Regulatory Authority and the Regulatory Authority shall coordinate with NDMO. The Data Controller shall obtain NDMO's approval – having coordinated with the Regulatory Authority – prior to sharing the personal data with other entities outside the Kingdom.'[49]

Presumably, the mechanism for extraterritorial data transfer approval will be contained within the forthcoming final implementing regulations to the PDPL. However, one should not assume that such licenses will be granted liberally, if at all. In this regard, the EU's General Data Protection Regulation restricts export of national personal data as well, but the process and legal authorization to do so are not standardized across the Union Simply prohibiting export rather than restricting export makes things simpler. For that reason, it is prudent to take Saudi Arabia at its word as expressed in Article 29 of its PDPL: export of non-anonymized Saudi personal data will not be permitted.

Extraterritoriality

By their terms, the PDIR applies to all entities in the Kingdom that process personal data as well as all entities outside the Kingdom that process personal data related to individuals residing in the Kingdom. Saudi regulations have always been territorial. The Kingdom does not try to impose its rules on foreign countries. The result is that national laws, while sometimes cosmetic, are often

---

[49] §5.4, PDIR

rigorously enforced. This is one of the first of the Kingdom's laws that claim extraterritorial jurisdiction. In most other cases, the Kingdom's laws only apply to activities within its national borders.

CHAPTER SIX

Data Export

Article 29 of the Law contains a specific provision on the transfer of personal data of Saudi citizens outside the Kingdom. It is worthwhile to set out at length the text of this article:

Except in cases of extreme necessity to preserve the life of the data owner outside the Kingdom of Saudi Arabia or his vital interests, or to prevent, examine or treat a disease infection, the controller may not transfer personal data outside the Kingdom or disclose it to a party outside the Kingdom of Saudi Arabia unless for implementation of an obligation under an agreement to which the Kingdom is a party, or to serve the interests of the Kingdom or for other purposes as determined by the regulations, after the following conditions are met:

1- Transfer or disclosure shall not prejudice national security or the vital interests of the Kingdom of Saudi Arabia.
2- Provide sufficient guarantees to maintain confidentiality of personal data that will be transferred or disclosed, so that the standards for protecting personal data shall not be less than the standards contained in the law and regulations.
3- The transfer or disclosure shall be limited to the minimum

amount of personal data that is needed.
4- Approval of the competent authority on the transfer or disclosure of data as determined by the regulations.

With the exception of the condition mentioned in Paragraph (1) of this Article, the competent authority may exempt the controller, in each case separately, from complying with one of the aforementioned conditions if the competent authority, alone or jointly with other parties, determine that the personal data will have an acceptable level of protection outside the Kingdom of Saudi Arabia, and that the data is not sensitive data.[50]

The last paragraph of Article 29 empowers SDAIA to grant exemptions to this broad prohibition on data transfer. By use of the "in each case separately" language, a fair reading of this article leads to the conclusion that each controller must individually request an exemption when data is to be sent outside the Kingdom. To our knowledge, the SDAIA has not yet established a procedure to request an exemption.

Also note that "sensitive data" is a term defined in the Law[51] and so the SDAIA's powers do not extend to exempting the transborder transfer of sensitive data.

Foreign controllers must appoint an in-Kingdom representative to liaise with the SDAIA.[52]

In short, the Law recognizes that Saudi personal data is transferred

---

[50] The original Arabic is just as confusing as the English, which suggests that the SDAIA can only exempt one of the four listed conditions. In our view, a more reasonable view is that the SDAIA may grant exemptions on an individual bases were all four conditions.

[51] Article 1(11). Sensitive data includes: ethnic, tribal, religious or political affiliation; group membership, criminal records or security information; biometric or genetic information, credit information, health, infant legitimacy or location information. It is not clear whether "location" information refers to individual addresses.

[52] Article 33(2). Application of this provision is temporarily suspended.

outside the Kingdom. A period of time has been given to the SDAIA to formulate implementing regulations so as to insure that such data is safeguarded. Under the Law, the controller[53] must identify those entities outside the Kingdom to which data might be "transferred, disclosed or processed." It makes little sense to require identification in the context of a blanket prohibition unless this provision is triggered where the SDAIA has granted an exemption.

As pointed out above, the CITC's policy discouraged transborder data transfer. Whether this policy will change with the transfer of jurisdiction to the SDAIA is an open question. The views of the Saudi Central Bank must also be taken into consideration. While it is no secret that banks outsource back office data processing to foreign companies overseas, it is also true that given notorious and highly-publicized leaks that the Kingdom views transborder transfers as inherently risky and will in the future aggressively move to onshore current practice.

Transfer of personal data of Saudi citizens outside the Kingdom is addressed as follows:

"Except in cases of extreme necessity to preserve the life of the data owner outside the Kingdom or his vital interests, or to prevent, examine or treat infection, the controller may not transfer personal data outside or disclose it to offshore parties except to fulfill obligations under international treaties, or to serve the national interest or for other purposes as determined by the regulations, except as follows:

Transfer or disclosure shall not prejudice national security or vital national interests.

Sufficient guarantees are provided to maintain confidentiality of such personal data, under standards not less than as set forth in the Law and Regulations.

Transfer or disclosure is limited to the minimum needed.

Approval of the competent authority on transfer or disclosure as set forth by Regulations.

Except as stated in Art. 1, the Authority may exempt controllers individually from these conditions if it acting alone or jointly with

---

[53] That is, data collector.

others determines that the personal data will be adequately protected, and is not sensitive."

The language "in each case separately" implies that controllers must request individual exemptions to send data abroad, a procedure that has yet to be defined.

"Sensitive data" is defined, and the SDAIA's powers do not extend to exempting its transborder transfer.

Foreign controllers must appoint an in-Kingdom representative to liaise with the SDAIA.

In short, the Law impliedly recognizes that Saudi personal data is currently commonly transferred outside the Kingdom, and the SDAIA has been given three years to issue regulations to protect such data, leaving it to the controller to identify those entities outside the Kingdom to which data might be "transferred, disclosed or processed."

It remains to be seen whether and to what extent the SDAIA will extend CITC's policy of discouraging transborder data transfer, and what position the Central Bank (SAMA) may take. While banks routinely outsource back-office data processing overseas, in the context of highly-publicized recent leaks transborder transfers are viewed as inherently risky, and hence a likely target for regulatory tightening.

CHAPTER SEVEN

Data Sharing Regulations

The Data Sharing Regulations[54] apply to the sharing or disclosure of government data. It does not apply to data in the private sector. The sharing of that data is subject to other rules.[55] The Data Sharing Regulations apply to the sharing or disclosure of collected government data with other government agencies as well as private entities.

Sharing among agencies is based on the following principles:

Principle 1: Data Sharing Culture

All Government entities act as a Single Source of Truth (SSOT) for the data they produce. Hence, entities shall request data from SSOTs directly to avoid its duplication, inaccuracy, and storage in multiple sources rather than recreating it themselves or requesting from third parties. If the request to share data is submitted to the entity that acts as a data custodian of Government data and is not its SSOT, then a permission to share from SSOT is mandatory.

---

[54] Data Sharing Regulations constitute Chapter 6 of the NDMO's National Data Governance Interim Regulations.

[55] Such as the requirement to protect sensitive personal data under the PDPL.

Principle 2: Clear Purpose for Data Sharing

The Data Requestor should clearly state the reason or legal basis behind the request for sharing data - except for data and entities exempted by a Royal Decree. Data should only be shared when it delivers a public benefit and would not inflict harm against national interests, organizations, individuals, or the environment.

Principle 3: Authorized Access

All parties involved in Data Sharing should have the appropriate authority (security clearance might be needed based on the nature and sensitivity of the data), knowledge, and skills along with properly trained staff to handle shared data.

Principle 4: Transparency

All parties involved in Data Sharing should make available all information that is necessary for the successful delivery of the Data Sharing purpose including required data, purpose behind data sharing request, data transfer and storage mechanism, data security controls, and data disposal mechanism.

Principle 5: Collective Accountability

All parties involved in Data Sharing should be held accountable for Data Sharing decisions, for processing it according to the defined purposes, and for taking the necessary actions to ensure data quality and implementation of security controls as defined in the Data Sharing agreement and as prescribed by relevant national laws and regulations.

Principle 6: Data Security

All parties involved in Data Sharing should have an adequate set of security controls to protect and safeguard data and enable a secure environment for Data Sharing in line with relevant national laws and regulations, and in line with the National Cybersecurity Authority requirements.

Principle 7: Ethical Data Use

All parties involved in Data Sharing should apply ethical practices throughout the Data Sharing process to ensure fairness, integrity, trust, and respect, and go beyond meeting data protection and security standards or other

regulatory requirements.[56]
These principles are outlined in the following graphic:

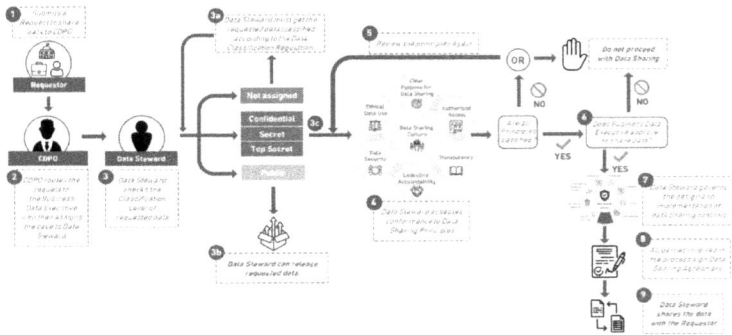

The regulations propose that the evaluation of requests for disclosure that meet all classification and protective requirements shall take place within thirty days. Disclosure of the data shall take place within 60 days after approval is given.[57]

Shared must be controlled and protected. In other words, data does not lose its classification due to its transfer to another government agency. Data does not lose its classification because of transfer to a private entity performing a government contract. According to the PDPL, sensitive personal data must in all cases be protected.

---

[56] §6.2
[57] §6.4

CHAPTER EIGHT

Freedom of Information

The Freedom of Information Interim Regulations[58] apply to all requests seeking access to public records. The Regulations make it clear that anyone may request information from a Saudi agency. No particular standing or interest is required.[59] However, requests may not be anonymously.[60] Certain information is exempt from disclosure, namely:

> 1. Information that, if disclosed, may harm the Kingdom of Saudi Arabia's national security, policies, interests or rights;
> 2. Military and security information;
> 3. Documents and information obtained in agreement with another state and classified as protected;
> 4. Inquiries, investigations, checks, inspections and monitoring in respect of a crime or violation;
> 5. Information that include recommendations, suggestions or consultations for issuing governmental

---

[58] Rules concerning access to Saudi government information by the public constitute chapter 7 of the National Data Governance Interim Regulations
[59] §7.3
[60] §7.4(4)

legislation or decision not issued yet;

    6.   Commercial, industrial, financial or economic information that, if disclosed, may result in gaining profits or avoiding losses in an illegitimate manner;

    7.   Scientific or technological searches or rights included intellectual property right that, if disclosed, may result in infringement of incorporeal right;

    8.   Tender and bidding information that, if disclosed, may give rise to violation of fair competition;

    9.   Information and the like, which are protected, confidential or personal under another law, or require certain legal action to be accessed or obtained.[61]

Otherwise, disclosure is subject to the following key principles:

Principle 1: Transparency
Individuals have the right to access information related to public entities,, activities to enhance integrity, transparency, and accountability.

Principle 2: Accountability and Reasonable Justification
Any restrictions on requesting access or obtaining protected information received, produced, or managed by public entities must be justified in a clear and explicit manner.

Principle 3: Public Information Disclosure
Every individual has the right to access or obtain public information – unprotected – and the applicant does not necessarily have a certain status or interest in this information to be able to obtain it and is not subject to any legal accountability related to this right.[62]

Applicants whose request is denied are entitled to be informed of

---

[61] §7.1
[62] §7.2

the reason for the denial and may appeal such denial.[63]

All requests for information are treated equally. Presumably, this would mean handling on a first-in, first-out basis. How different agencies will handle requests remains to be seen. Each agency is to establish a unit to handle information requests.[64] Note that the requirement to *disclose* information is not the same as a requirement for the agency to *create* new documents which issue opinions or which call for an agency interpretation of its own or other regulations. The disclosure of information is separate from the adjudicatory function. There is nothing in the regulations which require the regulator to regulate in a certain way.

Requests for government information must meet the following standards:

> The main requirements for the request to access public information :
> 1.   The request should be in writing or electronically;
> 2.   The request should be filled out in a dedicated form made accessible by the public entity;
> 3.   The request should clearly state that it is a request for Freedom of Information purposes;
> 4.   The request should give details about how notices can be sent to the requester (for example: address, email, or through the entity's website);
> 5.   The request should be sent directly to the public entity.[65]

There is nothing in these to require the government agency to redact personal or sensitive information prior to disclosure. However, §7.6 (2) ("General Dispositions") requires the agency to "balance the right to be informed and to access information with other necessary requirements, such as national security and personal data protection." This, along with the provisions of the PDPL, provide a basis for the agency to redact personal or sensitive data.

---

[63] §7.3
[64] §7.4(2)
[65] §7.5

* * *

Request for government information flowchart:

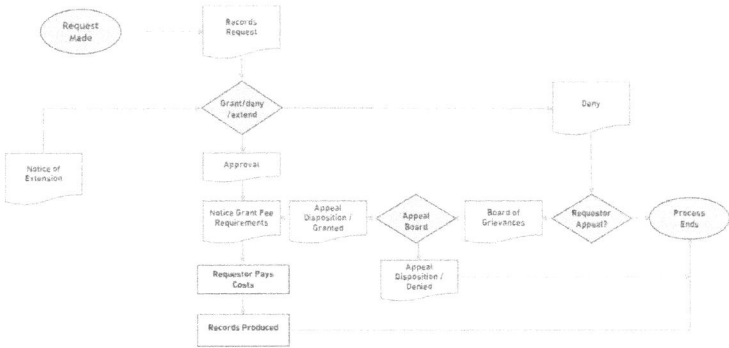

CHAPTER NINE

Open Data Interim Regulations

The Open Data Interim Regulations[66] cover all data collected or produced by government agencies. General principles concerning such data are as follows:

Principle 1: Open by Default

This principle ensures that the Government avail most of its data to the public by default unless there is sufficient justification that non-disclosure of data is of greater public interest.

Principle 2: Open Format and Machine-Readable

Datasets should be made publicly accessible in a machine-readable format that allows automated processing. Data should be stored in widely used file formats (such as CSV, XLS, JSON, XML) that facilitate machine processing.

Principle 3: Up to Date

Open datasets should be regularly published in their most recent state and should be made available to the public in a timely fashion. Whenever feasible, data collected by the Government should be released as quickly as it is gathered. Priority should be given to data

---

[66] The Open Data Interim Regulations constitute Chapter 8 of the National Data Governance Interim Regulations.

whose utility is time sensitive.

Principle 4: Comprehensive

Open datasets should be as complete and as granular as possible, reflecting what is recorded, in compliance with the National Data Privacy Regulation. Metadata that defines and explains the raw data should be included with explanations or formulas for how data was derived or calculated.

Principle 5: Non-discriminatory

Datasets shall be available to anyone without discrimination or requirement for registration. Any person should be able to access open data published at any time without having to identify him/herself or to provide justification for gaining access.

Principle 6: Free of Charge

Open data should be made available to the public free of charge.

Principle 7: KSA Open data License

Open data should be subject to the Kingdom,,s Open data License that provides the legal basis for Open data usage while defining the conditions, obligations, and restrictions applicable to the user. Any usage of Open data indicates acceptance of the License terms.

Principle 8: For Improved Governance and Citizen Engagement

Open data should enable informed civic participation and reinforce governments,, transparency and accountability to improve decision-making and enhance the provision of public services.

Principle 9: For Inclusive Development and Innovation

Entities should play an active role in promoting the reuse of Open data and providing the necessary supporting resources and expertise. Entities should actively work on empowering a future generation of Open data innovators and engaging individuals, organizations, and the general public in unlocking the value of Open data.

In line with these principles, data must first be classified. Once the data has been found to be publishable, it shall be made available to the public through the National Open Data Portal. Agencies must affirmatively publish Open Data. Disclosure of such public datasets is thus automatic and does not follow the Freedom of Information procedures outlined elsewhere in the National Policy document.

CHAPTER TEN

Data Protection

Personal data is, by definition, sensitive data. Under Article 5 of the National Data Protection Framework, the regulations apply to "all entities that process personal data as well as entities *outside the Kingdom* that process personal data relating to individuals residing in the Kingdom."

The Personal Data Protection Law (the "Law") entrusted regulation authority over private personal information to a new Saudi Data and Artificial Intelligence Authority ("SDAIA"), replacing the Communications and Information Technology Commission ("CITC") in this role over a two-year transitional period. CITC has required servers containing personal data to be located in Saudi Arabia, a policy which the SDAIA may or may not adopt depending on the content of as yet unpublished implementing regulations.

Entities that collect private information for storage and ("controllers") will now face restrictions, including data on Saudi residents by offshore entities, recognizing that such processing remains common despite the broad CITC prohibition.

A controller may only process personal data with the subject's written consent, except where performed pursuant to an existing agreement.

Controllers may not require consent as a condition for the service (except for data processing services), and may only collect data from individuals or "publicly available sources," which in the

Kingdom are evident only in the breach. No consent is required for scientific, research or statistical uses.

In conducting an initial audit, the following items must be considered:

1. Assets: What data do we have that must be protected?
2. Threats: Do we face any threats?
3. Vulnerabilities: Are systems secure?
4. Environments: Is the operating environment regularly patched?
5. Controls: What systems are in place?
6. Incident Response Planning: Devise a plan. 235[67]
   a. back-up
   b. reporting
   c. contacting[68]

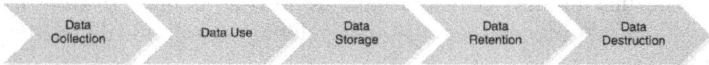

As part of the initial audit, the following areas should be examined, keeping in mind that 40% of the threats will be from internal, and not external actors:

1. Threat assessment: Competitors? Who would profit in case of a data breach?
2. Vulnerability assessment: How secure are the systems in place? How often are they tested?
3. Risk analysis: What would be the result of a data breach? To reputation, to the business to future expansion?
4. Risk register: A thorough list of all organizational risks.
5. Risk evaluation: Cost effectiveness of preventive action.
6. Risk assessment: Summary (to be made available to

---

[67] *Moschovitis*, p. 235

[68] *See,* Grama, *Legal and Privacy Issues in Information Security,* 3rd ed., Jones & Bartlett, (2022) at Ch. 1.

regulators)[69]

Personal data is, by definition, sensitive data. Under Article 5 of the National Data Protection Framework, the regulations apply to "all entities that process personal data as well as entities *outside the Kingdom that process personal data relating to individuals residing in the Kingdom.*"

Data Protection: Cloud Computing

A company that provides cloud computing services must register with the Communications and Information Technology Commission ("CITC"). This applies if the servers are in Saudi Arabia. Unclear if registration is required if data is collected and processed overseas. Nevertheless, National Data Framework protections apply even if CITC rules do not require registration.

Biometric Data

Biometric data is classified as "sensitive data" in Saudi Arabia. There are no special rules regarding the processing biometric data, but such data is protected as any other type of sensitive data.

Article (5/1) of the National Data Governance Policy issued by the National Data Management Office (NDMO) in 2020 outlined the main principles and general rules for the protection of personal data, explaining that the rule applies to all entities in the Kingdom that totally or partially process personal data, as well as external parties which processes personal data related to individuals residing in KSA, which is

---

[69] *Moschovitis*, p. 216-217

done via the Internet or any other means.

Article (5/2) set forth the main principles to be taken into account when using the data, as follows:

1. Responsibility: the control authority's privacy policies and procedures are defined and documented, approved by the entity's first official (or whoever he delegates), and published to all parties concerned with their application.

2. Transparency: prepare a notice on the privacy policies and procedures of the control authority specifying the purposes for which the personal data was processed in a specific, clear and explicit manner.

3. Choice and consent: define all possible options for the person with the personal data and obtain his consent (implicit or explicit) regarding his data collection, use or disclosure.

4. Limiting data collection: data collection be limited to the minimum amount of data that enables the achievement of the purposes specified in the privacy notice.

5. Limiting data use, retention and disposal: the processing of personal data be restricted to the purposes specified in the privacy notice for which the data subject gave his implicit or explicit consent, and to keep it as long as necessary to achieve the specified purposes or as required by the laws, regulations and policies in force in the Kingdom. Destroying them in a safe manner prevents leakage, loss, misappropriation, misuse, or unauthorized access by law.

6. Data Access: define and provide the means by which the data owner can access his personal data for review, update and correction.

7. Limit disclosure of data: disclosure of personal data to external parties is restricted to the purposes specified in the privacy notice for which the data owner provided his implicit or explicit consent.

8. Data security: personal data is protected from leakage, damage, loss, misappropriation, misuse, modification or unauthorized access - according to what is issued by the National Cybersecurity Authority and the competent authorities.

9. Data quality: the personal data is kept accurate, complete and directly related to the purposes specified in the privacy notice.

10. Monitoring and Compliance: To monitor compliance with the privacy policy and procedures of the controller, handle inquiries, complaints and disputes related to privacy.

Under the Anti-Cybercrime Law[70]'s Article 6, material impinging on personal privacy is a violation. This law covers publication of personal information, including photographs, without the consent of the data subject.

The penalty for an Article 6 violation is a maximum of five years in prison or a three million SAR fine.

---

[70] Cybercrime Law: Royal Decree No. M/17, 8 Rabi 1 1428, 26 March 2007

CHAPTER ELEVEN
Cybersecurity Controls

The NCA "developed the Essential Cybersecurity Controls (ECC-1: 2018) (ECC) to set the minimum cybersecurity requirements for national organizations." This document outlines general cybersecurity requirements for government agencies in the Kingdom and is supplemented by the Social Media and Teleworking Controls.

The TCC applies to government agencies and private entities operating critical national infrastructure. It does not apply to private companies that merely process government data. Such companies are nonetheless encouraged to implement the ECC.

To assist in implementation, the NCA has created a tool to measure compliance with the requirements of the ECC. The bilingual tool can be downloaded from the agency's website.

The ECC requires the establishment of a dedicated cybersecurity function within each agency. Cybersecurity must not merely be an adjunct to an existing IT department but must be separate. The NCA recommends that the head of this department report directly to the agency head.

Essentially, the agency requires that cybersecurity be a component of all agency activity. This only makes sense as the use of unconnected devices has been deprecated. Often, the first act of any employee arriving at the workplace is logging in to the system. A potential disaster is likely if that system is not secure. The ECC requires a vulnerability assessment and remediation and conducting a configurations' review, securing configuration and hardening and patching, that is, testing before going live with changes.

Software to be used by the government must also be secure:

1. Using secure coding standards.
2. Using trusted and licensed sources for software development tools and libraries.
3. Conducting compliance test for software against the defined organizational cybersecurity requirements.
4. Secure integration between software components.
5. Conducting a configurations' review, secure configuration and hardening and patching before going live for software products.

Periodic reviews and audits are essential. Even though the ECC does not by its terms apply to private companies, the personal information of agency contractors must be protected. *See, ECC Cybersecurity in Human Resources §1.9 at p.17.* There may be no post-employment access to agency systems.

An employee awareness program should be implemented to include the following:

1. Secure handling of email services, especially phishing emails. Secure handling of mobile devices and storage media.
2. Secure Internet browsing.
3. Secure use of social media.

Defense mechanisms must include:

1. User authentication based on username and password.
2. Multi-factor authentication for remote access.
3. User authorization based on identity and access control principles: Need-to-Know and Need-to-Use, Least Privilege and Segregation of Duties.
4. Privileged access management.
5. Periodic review of users' identities and access rights.

* * *

Agency data protection systems must include the following:

1.   Advanced, up-to-date and secure management of malware and virus protection on servers and workstations.
2.   Restricted use and secure handling of external storage media.
3.   Patch management for information systems, software and devices.
4.   Centralized clock synchronization with an accurate and trusted source (e.g., Saudi Standards, Metrology and Quality Organization (SASO)).
5.   Requirements reviewed periodically

Email protection methods are to include the following:

1.   Analyzing and filtering email messages (specifically phishing emails and spam) using advanced and up-to-date email protection techniques.
2.   Multi-factor authentication for remote and webmail access to email service.
3.   Email archiving and backup.
4.   Secure management and protection against Advanced Persistent Threats (APT), which normally utilize zero-day viruses and malware.
5.   Validation of the organization's email service domains (e.g., using Sender Policy Framework (SPF)).

Remediation of potential vulnerabilities and penetration testing are essential components of the ECC. Penetration testing is conducting a simulated cyberattack against your own systems.[71] Not all of the requirements are in cyberspace. Physical requirements are also covered:

1.   Authorized access to sensitive areas within the organization (e.g., data center, disaster recovery center, sensitive information processing facilities, security surveillance center, network cabinets).

---

[71] *Moschovitis,* p. 282

2.   Facility entry/exit records and CCTV monitoring. Protection of facility entry/exit and surveillance records.
3.   Secure destruction and re-use of physical assets that hold classified information (including documents and storage media).
4.   Security of devices and equipment inside and outside the organization's facilities.

In view of Iran's attack against Saudi Aramco[72] and to prevent similar attacks in the future, the following guidelines are implemented in the ECC:

1.   Strict physical and virtual segmentation when connecting industrial production networks to other networks within the organization (e.g., corporate network).
2.   Strict physical and virtual segmentation when connecting systems and industrial networks with external networks (e.g., Internet, wireless, remote access).
3.   Continuous monitoring and activation of cybersecurity event logs on the industrial networks and its connections.
4.   Isolation of Safety Instrumental Systems (SIS).
5.   Strict limitation on the use of external storage media.
6.   Strict limitation on connecting mobile devices to industrial production networks.
7.   Periodic review and secure configuration and hardening of industrial, automated, support systems, and devices.
8.   Vulnerability management for industrial control systems and operational technology (ICS/OT).
9.   Patch management for industrial control systems and operational technology (ICS/OT).
10.   Cybersecurity applications management related to the protection of the industrial systems from viruses and malware.

---

[72] Following the Stuxnet attack against Iran's uranium-enriching centrifuges, in 2012 Saudi Aramco was attacked with a similar cyber weapon.

CHAPTER TWELVE

Cybercrime

Saudi Arabia enacted legislation to address the issue of cybercrime in 2007.[73] As with most criminal laws, the law is designed to be comprehensive in the area of its subject matter. Enhancing privacy, though, is not one of the stated goals of the law. However the law prohibits the interception of data which is then used to spy on a person in order to blackmail him or force him to take unwanted action. The law also prohibits invasions of privacy achieved through the use of mobile phones "and the like." The law prohibits unauthorized access to computer systems as well as improperly accessing bank or financial data.

Accessing computer systems in order to leak data is prohibited, as is the "production, preparation, transmission or storage" of matter which impinges on an individual's privacy. So even though protected privacy is not one of the stated goals of the law, the law criminalizes acts which infringe upon an individual's right to privacy, including financial privacy.

The CITC is to lend technical support to the Bureau of of Investigation and Public Prosecution to monitor violations of the Anti-Cybercrime law. The Saudi Anti-Cybercrime Law[1] comprehensively defines cybercrimes. While the CITC is

---

[73] Anti-Cybercrime Law, Royal Decree M/17, 8 /3/1428, March 26, 2007.

authorized to provide technical assistance to law enforcement, it lacks express authority to shut down an app or web page on its own.

CHAPTER THIRTEEN
Prepare for the PDPL

Consider GDPR Compliance

Based on Saudi Arabia's existing data security and privacy legislation, it is fair to say that Saudi Arabia is following an enhanced version of the GDPR. Up until now, the GDPR has too often been seen as a "Europe only" law which other countries, such as the United States were free to ignore.

Because US law generally requires a finding of actual harm prior to the grant of any compensation, companies faced no risks from their American customers and only had to worry about fines from regulators. These could not be ignored, as sometimes these fines were substantial.

Despite the fines, few companies made any substantive efforts to follow the European lead, though increasingly, the need to do business outside the USA means that those who thought privacy compliance is optional only find that position is simply not sustainable not only outside, but even inside the US.

In 2020 in a landmark but relatively unrecognized decision of the European Court of Justice, the United States was classified as a territory where privacy rights are not respected. More particularly, "cloud services hosted in the US are incapable of complying with the GDPR and EU privacy laws." Companies that continue to do business with non-compliant American companies risk serious fines.

The GDPR closely tracks what we know of Saudi legislation, so compliance with one is a substantial stride towards compliance with the other.

Though it is still not clear what a company must specifically do to insure compliance with Saudi Arabia's PDPL, companies that are already compliant with the GDPR will likely find that they are already very close to compliance with the new Saudi regulations.

Since what is required to be GDPR compliant is already well-known, starting with GDPR compliance is good way to prepare for Saudi compliance.

Preparing for the PDPL

1. Who is covered?

Everyone. Every single company keeps personal information concerning its employees. This means, logically, that every company is covered under the law. It also means that a new national registry of companies will be created pursuant to the law. It also means that a new tax, in the guise of SDAIA registration, may be required.

Some have claimed that this is too broad, that the data privacy laws were not intended to be so broad so as to apply to every single business in the country. The counterargument is a strong one:

> "Now, you might argue that there is no business that does not collect PII. How can you be in business and not collect some personally identifiable information? How do you bill your client? Obviously, you have the client's PII."[74]

* * *

---

[74] *Moschovitis*, 50

The same is true for every Saudi government agency, no matter its size or jurisdiction. The subject of government is the governed. The governed are identified by their personal data. It is impossible to enforce or even consider laws without such information.

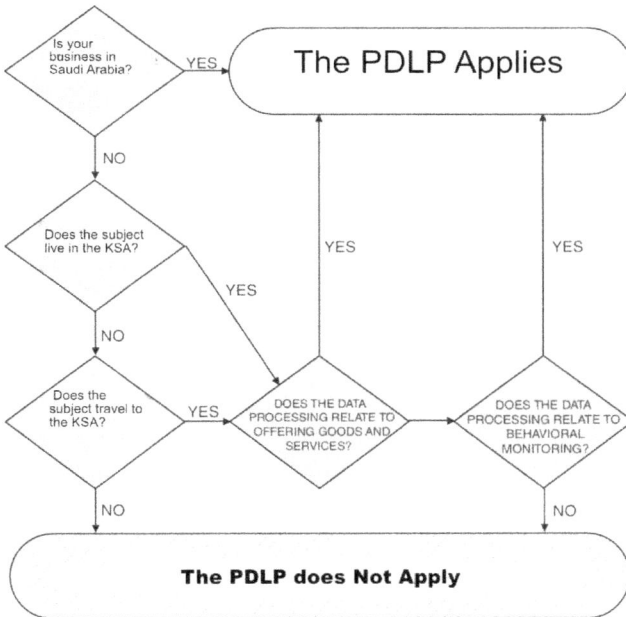

The cost of SDAIA registration and who has to register need clarification. Requiring a small business with just a few employees to pay SAR 100,000 to register is unthinkable and politically unworkable. It is likely then, that there will be graduated registration costs. But this carries risks because then larger companies will claim that they are discriminated against. That SDAIA would exempt smaller companies in the forthcoming regulations carries its own risks, since an individual's privacy rights should not depend on the size of his employer's workforce.

Since an audit of compliance policies will mostly be done on-line and will be software-based, it should cost SDAIA no more to audit a large company than a small one. It is not clear then, how SDAIA will resolve this dilemma.

2. Appoint a Data Controller

Every reporting entity must have a data controller under the law. This data controller may perform other functions in the reporting company. The data controller will be responsible for liaising with SDAIA and insuring that the company is compliant.

3. Audit of Personal Data

A company must determine *what* data it maintains on its employees, customers and others; it must also determine *where* this data is kept, whether in a database, a file cabinet, a journal or lose papers in a manager's desk.

The company must then determine *why* such data is collected; and *whether* such data is disclosed or transferred outside the organization.

All company contracts must be reviewed in order to determine if there are any privacy issues raised. Many contracts will obtain personal information about individuals. The existence of such information should be noted, redacted where possible—e.g. individual passport numbers of managers need not be disclosed except where required by an official request—and entered into the company's privacy or compliance database.

The company must ask the following questions:

1. Is PII information in any form collected?
2. What kind of PII is collected?
3. What is the number of such records collected?
4. How long is PII retained?
5. How is PII removed?
6. What is the purpose of collecting PII?

7. Is PII transferred to others?[75]

Once this information is gathered, it should be entered into a company privacy database.

4. Privacy Database

The answers to these questions should be kept in a new privacy database to facilitate submission to SDAIA for compliance purposes. A memorial of the method used for obtaining consent to disclose and proof of such consent should be contained here as well.

5. Establish Policies

A company privacy policy should be drafted and implemented company-wide. The policy must be communicated to all those from whom data is collected. The company will have to change existing procedures in order to achieve compliance with the PDPL.

6. Foreign Transfer

Companies that routinely transfer personal data relating to Saudi citizens must immediately review the need for such transfer and desist from the practice since such transfers will be greatly restricted once the PDPL takes effect. It remains to be seen whether SDAIA will care out any exceptions to the general prohibition on extraterritorial data transfer.

Rights Afforded

The GDPR recognizes a collection of rights under the law, including the following:

1	Right to be informed
2	Right of access

---

[75] *Moschovitis*, 52

3	Right to erasure
4	Right to rectification
5	Right to data portability
6	Right to object
7	Right to withdraw consent

If you are GDPR compliant, you are almost compliant with the PDPL. Both laws require the appointment of a Data Controller and advice of the appointment to the regulator. If a Data Protection Officer is appointed, this information must also be transmitted.

Controller		Data Protection Officer
Name		
Address		
E-mail		
Telephone		

An inventory of the data held by the company must be conducted, categorized and provided to the regulator, including but not limited to the following areas:

Business Function	
Purpose of Processing	
Controller	
Categories of Individuals	
Categories of Personal Data	
Retention Schedule	
G'ral Description of Security Measures	* * *

Reason for Processing
Personal Data
Privacy Notices
Consent
Location of Personal Data
Breaches

It is likely that SDAIA may draft its own forms for submission of the information mentioned above for reporting purposes.

CHAPTER FOURTEEN
Digital Economy Policy

Saudi Arabia published its *Digital Economy Policy*[76] whose purpose is to "inform[ing} the public sector, private enterprises and the international community of the Kingdom's position on matters related to the digital economy."

The policy "sets out guiding principles for government agencies to leverage the digital economy…to drive diversification and sustainability across the economy and create a more competitive advantage…"

The policy then sets forth the Kingdom's position with respect to these matters.

High quality, dependable affordable and universal internet access is the first of these. In order to accomplish this goal, the Kingdom will establish Lish strategic partnerships with private service providers. Strict compliance with Kingdom regulations is required of these providers to protect society from potential harm. Kingdom spending in these areas will focus on meeting these goals.

As part of its policy, the Kingdom encourages data collection, effective use and sharing of open data. This is a new development, given Saudi Arabia's historical respect for privacy. To ease the

---

[76] *Digital Economy Policy in the Kingdom of Saudi Arabia,* published by the Digital Transformation Unit of the Ministry of Communications and Information Technology, retrieved from the agency's website.

burden on data providers, the Kingdom is trying to establish a "once only" policy, in which different government agencies will share data rather than collecting it on multiple occasions from citizens and residents.

The use of digital platforms has become ubiquitous in Saudi Arabia, with many Saudi agencies taking advantage of the pandemic not only to go paperless but to entirely transact business on bespoke Internet applications. Unfortunately, integration of all these new platforms is a work in progress.

The Kingdom is open to innovation and adopting new technologies in order to ease the friction between the governed and the government and to generally improve the country's quality of life.

Affording job opportunities to the disabled in the digital realm is a reachable goal.

Some goals seem to conflict with the Kingdom's trade policies. For example, despite WTO membership, certain sections of the economy are not fully open to foreign investment. The Kingdom seeks digital open markets while "real-life" markets are not fully open. Inevitably there will be friction. In general though, the Kingdom seeks to be a strong backer of digital tools to enhance commercial and private lives.

CHAPTER FIFTEEN

Cloud Computing

Council of Ministers Resolution No. (292), dated 27/04/1441H, in Article Seven, affirmed the continuation of the Ministry of Communications and Information Technology and CITC in accordance with its powers stipulated in the Act and CITC's Statute in regulating the matters related to information technology, such as cloud computing.[77]

The CITC established the national Cloud Computing Regulatory Framework as a set of guidelines for the use of cloud computing in Saudi Arabia. The rules apply to cloud computing services afforded to anyone resident in or with a residence address in Saudi Arabia.[78] Datacenters located in the Kingdom are also subject to the CCRF.[79] Cloud service providers must register with and be licensed by the CCIT.

Cloud computing has been defined as "the delivery of hosted digital services, on demand, over a network, and commonly over the Internet." (*Moschovitis*, ibid. at p. 178)

The Cloud Computing Regulatory Framework does *not* apply to the collection of certain personal information alone since Section

---

[77] Cloud Computing Regulatory Framework, v.3.0, §1-3.

[78] §3-1-1, CCRF
[79] §3-1-2, CCRF

2-2-2 states:

> The mere storage and processing of [a] Subscriber's information (such as name, contact details or information on past transactions) by a person who provides services to these customers other than Cloud Computing Services does not constitute a cloud computing service.

A "Cloud Provider" is defined as "any Person providing Cloud Services to the public (entity or individual) through Datacenters it owns and/or manages itself, in whole or in part."[80]

The Kingdom's "Cloud First" cloud computing policy was first issued in February, 2019 by the CITC. The "Cloud First" policy is "meant to define and typically stimulate public sector migration from traditional IT solutions to cloud-based models."[81]

This policy applies only to government entities. It remains to be seen whether the government intends to lead by example in this space, or merely seeks to obtain efficiencies and reduce duplication of efforts by bringing in servers across dozens of Saudi agencies into centrally managed single cloud facilities. To achieve this goal, government agencies are prohibited from investing in data center infrastructure unless exempted from the cloud computing policy. Government agencies are to first consider approved government cloud service providers unless the data to be housed contains classified national defense information.

To this end, additional protections will be required of approved cloud service providers to enhance security for government-collected data.

The National Information Center will be the primary cloud service provider for the Kingdom of Saudi Arabia.

The Kingdom's Policy provides a more granular definition of what constitutes cloud computing:

> Cloud computing is a model which enables convenient, on-demand network access to a shared pool of configurable computing resources (e.g. networks, servers, storage, applications and services) that can be rapidly provisioned and released with minimal management effort or service

---

[80] §2-2-3-1, Cloud Computing Regulatory Framework

[81] CITC, Cloud First Policy at pg.7

provided interactions.[82]
Further,

> Cloud computing, at its core, offers three different services
> models, which provide applications, platforms and
> infrastructure as a service.

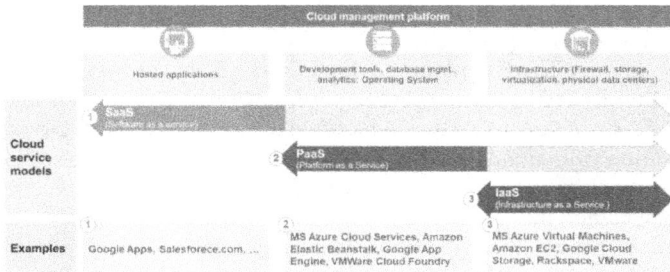

One of the goals of moving to cloud-based platforms is to achieve
greater security:

> Cloud services typically offer a high level of cyber security
> that is difficult to be attained by governmental entities
> themselves [since] leading cloud service providers have
> been shown to invest significantly in cyber security-related
> R&D activities.[83]

The Cloud First Policy recognizes the transformative nature of
cloud computing, noting that "the way we order a cab, the way we
order food, communication with other people, meeting, etc." have
all been changed because of the cloud. Given the previous
regulation of these sectors by agencies such as the Ministry of
Transportation, it is noteworthy that Saudi Arabia does not seek ro
resist technology-driven change but instead welcomes it.

---

[82] CITC, "KSA Cloud First Policy, Feb. 2019, quoting the definition issued
by the National institute of Standards and Technology.
[83] CITC, Cloud First Policy at p. 8.

Just as important, cloud computing will reduce government spending. Currently, Saudi government entities support over four hundred poorly utilized data centers. Most of these can be consolidated, gaining at once greater security and lower costs.

Also, responsibility for cyber-security has been spread among all of these data centers. A move to the cloud will centralize and increase the security of collected data.

As part of efforts to lead by example, even though the CFP only applies to government agencies, the CITC believes that:

> [T]he impact of cloud computing will go beyond the government IT sector, it will accelerate the digital transformation in the Kingdom through pushing adoption of leading technologies such as Artificial Intelligence [and] 4th Industrial Revolution technologies.

The immediate goal, though, is to "help the government move from traditional IT services …to faster, more automated e-services."

It is important to note that neither the Cloud First Policy or the Cloud Computing Regulatory Framework impose any requirements on the private sector per se, though interaction with the government increasingly will be through cloud based platforms and interfaces.

As part of the cloud initiative, the government will classify all data it holds. The National Data Office will play a role and must approve the classification of any data as "Restricted."

The policy also provides guidelines for government agencies seeking to upgrade or invest in their current digital infrastructure.

A company that provides cloud computing services must register with the CITC. This applies if the servers are in Saudi Arabia. It is unclear if registration is required if data is collected and processed overseas. Nevertheless, National Data Framework protections apply even if CITC rules do not require registration.

Cloud Cybersecurity Controls

The National Cybersecurity Authority regulates "the development of cybersecurity national policies, governance mechanisms, frameworks, standards controls and guidelines to support the role… of cybersecurity which has increased with the rise of security risks in cyberspace."

The growth of cloud computing, according to the NCA, means new cybersecurity risks. To this end, the NCA publishers new Cybersecurity Controls to be implemented by cloud providers. The new controls are a study of best practices globally, including those implemented by such countries as Germany, Singapore and the United States.

The goal of the new controls is to protect the "confidentiality, integrity and availability of data and information within the cloud environment." As such, privacy is a key component. The Controls are required by all Saudi cloud computing service providers.

It is important to note that the Controls are both managerial, the is, relating to governance, as well as technical. Managerial controls such as, restricting access to generic account credentials are coupled with technical controls, such as secure session management, multi-factor authentication and the establishment of multi-factor authentication to thwart unauthorized log-in attempts. Monitoring traffic across external networks in order to detect anomalies is another part of maintaining security in the cloud.

Cloud service providers must inform subscribers, the NCA and the CITC of any data breach without "undue delay."[84] Cybersecurity controls are required of cloud service providers. Third-parties may not access subscriber data[85] without express written consent.[86] Subscribers must also be able to access, verify, correct or delete their data in the cloud at any time.[87] With some exceptions, liability for violations of the CCRF and its cybersecurity

---

[84] §3-3-11, CCRF
[85] §3-4-2-1, CCRF
[86] §3-4-3-2, CCRF.
[87] §3-4-4

provisions may not be excluded by contract.[88] Liquidated damages are permitted.

Saudi Arabia censors the Internet by blacklisting objectionable web sites. More than 500,000 have been blocked and cannot be accessed from the Kingdom without using elaborate technological work-arounds. However, content kept in the cloud and not accessible to the public is not subject to the Kingdom's content filtering rules, but will be removed if determined to be otherwise illegal.[89] Content that violates intellectual property laws is subject to removal. The Saudi Authority for Intellectual Property (SAIP) has jurisdiction over such issues, and under the CCRF, cloud service providers must honor orders issued by this agency.

Cloud Computing and Social Media

Saudi agencies have over the past several years come to rely on social media to communicate with customers and other stakeholders. Social media has become so convenient that it is often the only means to quickly communicate with an agency as for some reason, e-mails are all too often and routinely ignored. This is unlikely an official policy, but posting information on social media is akin to a limited broadcast, whereas e-mail--unless there is a list, only reaches a single individual.

Thus, in 2021 the National Cybersecurity Authority issue controls "to se the minimum cybersecurity requirements to enable agencies to use social media in a safe manner.

The Controls (OSMACC-1:2021) are mandatory and apply to Saudi government agencies. Private companies that operate sensitive national infrastructure must also comply with the Controls. The Controls aim to:

- Contribute to raising the level of cybersecurity at a national level

---

[88] §3-7-2 CCRF
[89] §3-9-1 CCRF

- Enabling organizations to use social media in a safe manner
- Readiness to respond effectively to cyber incidents that may have negative impacts

Social media controls further require providers to implement:

- Non-disclosure clauses and secure removal of organization's data by the third-party upon service termination.
- Communication procedures to report vulnerabilities and cyber incidents.
- Requirements for the third-party to comply with cybersecurity requirements and policies to protect organizations' social media accounts, and related laws and regulation.

This is accomplished by the following:

- Using social media accounts designated for organizations, not individuals.
- Registering using official information (official specific social media email and official mobile number), and do not use personal information.
- Verifying organization's social media accounts whenever possible and maintaining a consistent identity across all organization's social media accounts used; to facilitate knowledge of official accounts, and to discover fraud or unofficial accounts.
- Using a secure and specific password for each organization's social media account, changing the password regularly, and not to repeat the use of the same password.
- Using multi-factor authentication for organization's social media accounts logins.
- Activating and updating security questions and documenting them in a safe place.
- Managing organization's social media accounts access

rights based on business need, considering the sensitivity of the accounts, the level of access rights and the type of devices and systems used.

- Restricting access rights of service providers of social media manage- ment, social media monitoring or brand protection.
- Restricting access to organization's social media accounts to specific devices.

The last control is significant since at this time, an entire agency's access to its own social media account is through a mobile phone linked to an individual. While the second control prohibits the use of personal information in order to register an account, in practice this has been the exception rather than the rule. The situation is arguably worse in the private sector, where accounts are always linked to individuals and no official leverage can be brought to bear to recover accounts where an employee has left service.

Regular monitoring of activity on social media accounts is one approved method to insure that all posts are authorized. Restricting feature activation and frequent review of default configurations are also advised.

Cloud Computing and Teleworking

With respect to teleworking, the National Cybersecurity Authority issued another set of controls (TCC-1:2021), which require the location of the hosted telework systems to be inside the Kingdom of Saudi Arabia.[90]

Cloud Computing and Outsourcing

A company that seeks to outsource cloud computing services must

---

[90] TCC-1:2021 §3-1-1-1

insure that the provider is itself security-compliant. There is an alphabet soup list of various standards, such as CSA STAR, HIPAA, ISO27001, PCI-DSS, SAS-70, SOC-3, and TRUSTe. There is also the Cloud Security Alliance's STAR certification. Privacy Shield is another which is compliant with the GDPR and so is of particular interest to cloud customers in Saudi Arabia.[91]

A valuable resource is ENISA's Cloud Security Guide for SMEs —Cloud computing security risks and opportunities for SMEs— dated April 2015.

Cloud Computing Licensing

Those to seek to provide cloud services in Saudi Arabia must be registered, that is, licensed by the CITC. Licensing upon registration is not automatic. The CITC must approve the application of each applicant. A company which is to provide cloud service in Saudi Arabia must locate its servers within the Kingdom. If necessary hardware cannot be acquired in the Kingdom, the applicant must also apply to the CITC for permission to import any telecommunications or electronic equipment. The application process for Customs approval following CITC vetting of the equipment sought to be brought in is beyond the scope of this book, but can be found elsewhere.[92]

The application must identify the type of services to be provided, the applicant's experience of providing them and the technical standards which will be met.[93] The application must be submitted in Arabic, but supporting documentation such as technical manuals, may be submitted in English.

---

[91] Moschovitis, *ibid.* at p. 291.

[92] See O'Kane *Saudi Arabia Export Guide*, ISBN ISBN: 978-1-945979-13-2, Andalus Publishing (2022)

[93] The technical requirements are set forth in a CITC publication entitled, *Guide for Cloud Computing Service Providers in the Kingdom of Saudi Arabia,* v.4 (2021)

CHAPTER SIXTEEN

Cybersecurity

Cybersecurity has been defined as "the ongoing application of best practices intended to insure and preserve confidentiality, integrity and availability of digital information as wellas the safety of people and environments."[94]

Standards for cybersecurity have been issued by international, national and private-sector bodies. Among the growing number are the following:

1. The European Telecommunications Standards Institute (ETSI) TR 103 family of standards;

2. The IASME standards for small and medium-sized enterprises (IASME stands for Information Assurance for Small and Medium- sized Enterprises);

3. The Information Security Forum (ISF) Standard of Good Practice (SoGP);

4. The International Society for Automation (ISA) ISA62443 standards for industrial automation and control systems;

5. The Internet Engineering Task Force (IETF) via their Request for Comments (RFC) 2196 memorandum;

---

[94] *Moschovitis,* p.182

6. The Information Systems Audit and Control Association, now known only as ISACA, through their COBIT framework and Cybersecurity Nexus (CSX) resources;

7. The Institute for Security and Open Methodologies (ISECOM) with their Open Source Security Testing Methodology Manual (OSSTMM) and the Open Source Cybersecurity Playbook;

8. The ISO 27000 family of standards (ISO 27000–ISO27999);

9. The National Institute of Standards and Technology (NIST) Cyber-

security Framework (CSF); and

10. The North American Electric Reliability Corporation (NERC),

which via its Critical Infrastructure Protection (CIP) family of standards addresses electric systems and network security.[95]

In the broad sense there are two, and only two, kinds of threats: external and internal. 263 If you think that threats are only theoretical or happen to someone else, take a look at https://www.cvedetails.com, a list of commonly-used programs and their vulnerabilities. Thought to be innocuous, Zoom calls can open a pathway into secure systems. https://www.cvedetails.com/product/56977/?q=Zoom

Internal threats can never be eliminated entirely. Regular monitoring of systems and access, and identification of employee access on a "need to know" basis are essential. Among the other recommended steps a company can take are the following:

"1. Create legally binding agreements with employees and their use of equipment accessing corporate assets.

2. Create and communicate clear policies, standards, procedures, guide- lines for all information technology use and corporate systems access.

---

[95] *Moschovitis,* p. 186.

3. Have clear and timely onboarding and offboarding processes for all

employees.

4. Provide cybersecurity awareness training to all employees, at least

quarterly, and maintain awareness throughout the year.

5. Deploy a wide range of controls, including a well-tuned security information and event management system and a data loss protection system."[96]

---

[96] Moschovitis, p.300

CHAPTER SEVENTEEN
Mobile Phones

Rules concerning the protection of personal information have become ubiquitous and so are found in many different laws. Telecommunications providers must comply with CITC regulations with respect to maintaining the privacy of users' personal data.[97] For example, the CITC issued regulations concerning the provision of mobile phone service and the relationship between network providers and their customers. Paragraph 18 of the preamble of that document defines personal information:

> "Personal information" means every statement - whatever its source or form – that would specifically lead to recognize the user, or make him directly or indirectly identifiable, including a name, personal identification number, address, contact details, license number, personal records and property, bank account number or credit card, a user's static or animated image, and other data of a personal nature.

Given that this is a CITC regulation, at the very least this suggests that the term is to be given as broad a definition as possible.

* * *

---

[97] Regulations on the Protection of Rights of ICT Services' Users and on the Terms Of ICT Service Provision (RPRICT), v.1.0, Art. 14.

Article 8 of that regulation requires the collection of personal data before providing network access to a customer. Article 14 addresses privacy:

1. Service providers must abide by the regulations and decisions issued by the Commission or any other specialized competent authority, with regard to maintaining the privacy of users' personal data.

2. Service providers must treat all user data as confidential, and must protect them and take all necessary measures to prevent their infiltration, destruction, loss, embezzlement, usage, handling, modification or unauthorized access in violation of this document or any related Commission statute.

3. Service providers must maintain the confidentiality of communications and data sent or received through their public telecommunications networks and shall not allow any of their employees, affiliates or other parties to view, listen to or record them except in accordance with legal justifications.

Violations of these privacy policies may be made in the first instance to the network provider and then to the CITC. If the matter is not resolved, the CITC may refer the matter to the Telecommunications Bylaws Violation Committee.[98] However, in its Article 28 the consumer is permitted to seek compensation through the courts or the country's administrative committees. At present, given the lack of statutory damages, this enforcement provision neither punishes network providers nor compensates their customers. The network provider must retain records for a twelve month period.

Finally the CITC is given the authority to take "any measure it deems appropriate" for violations of this regulation. Presumably, this includes the power to fine or order compensation for those whose privacy has been breached.[99]

---

[98] RPRICT, *ibid.* Art.24(17).
[99] RPRICT, *ibid.* Art.28(4).

CHAPTER EIGHTEEN
Banking

The Saudi Arabian Monetary Authority (SAMA) in 2013 issued a document titled, "Banking Consumer Protection Principles." Article 9 of this document deals with the protection of consumer data. Article 9 imposes on banks the responsibility of safeguarding and maintaining the confidentiality of consumer data. The Article provides as follows:

> 9.1 A bank has [the] responsibility to protect consumer data and maintain the confidentiality of the data, including when it is held by a third party.
> 9.2 A bank shall provide a safe and confidential environment in all of its delivery channels to ensure the confidentiality and privacy of consumer data.
> 9.3 A bank has a general duty of confidentiality towards a customer except:
> --when a disclosure is imposed by the relevant authority (such as the Ministry of Interior, Courts, etc.)
> --when disclosure is made with the written consent of the consumer.
> 9.4 A bank shall have sufficient procedures, system controls and checks and employee awareness to protect consumer information and to identify and resolve any causes of information security breaches, where they may occur in the future.

> 9.5 A bank shall insure that the personal information of consumers can be acessed and used by authorized employees only. This is to insure that access to [a} consumer's financial and/or personal information is for authorized employees only, whether on the job or after they have ceased working for the bank.

Accessing a bank customer's personal information without authorization is a violation of Article 4 of the Anti-Cyber Crime Law.[100]

Fintech

The CITC issued regulations to govern new financial technology products. Fintech is defined by Investopedia as, "technology that seeks to improve and automate the delivery and use of financial services.[101] The CITC's Resolution No. 415 defines personal data[102] processing as including the collection of data from individuals and requires that each proposed service conduct a "Privacy Impact Assessment," a study which

> …aims to identify and assess the impact of that service or product on the privacy of personal data of new or current customers, including the specification of the required data, the description of the processing of the data, the scope and nature of the processing and an identification and assessment of privacy risks and treatment plans.

The results of the Privacy Impact Assessment must be transmitted to

---

[100] Royal Decree No. M/17 8/3/1428 (26 Mar.2007)

[101] https://www.investopedia.com/terms/f/fintech.asp

[102] Any information, regardless of its source or form, which would lead to identifying the customer, or that would render the customer identifiable directly or indirectly, including, but not limited to, names, ID numbers, addresses, contact numbers, licenses and registrations numbers and personal properties, bank account numbers and credit cards numbers, customer's photos or videos, as well as any other data of personal nature.

the CITC five days prior to the launch of any Fintech product. The proposed assessment must be submitted 21 days in advance and CITC approval must be obtained before the launch of any product. The CITC's Regulation 415 applies not only to Fintech, but any service or product based on an individual's personal data.

SAMA is also active in the Fintech regulatory space, providing a sandboxed initial test platform for the trial of new Fintech products.

CHAPTER NINETEEN
E-Commerce

The E-Commerce Law also contains privacy protections. Internet merchants must:

- protect consumer data
- not retain such data beyond the time necessary to conduct the transaction
- not retain such data except in order to process the transaction
- must keep the consumer's data registered through a portal until the consumer closes his account; and
- in case of a breach, advise the Ministry of Commerce within three days

Merchants who violate these provisions may be banned, receive a warning or a fine not to exceed SAR 1 million.Under Article 5 of the E-Commerce Implementing Regulations issued by the Ministry of Commerce, any data that leads to specific knowledge of the consumer's identity is considered protected Personal Consumer Data. This includes:

1. Names
2. Identity information
3. Addresses
4. Contact numbers

5. License numbers
6. Records and personal property
7. Account and bank card number
8. Still and moving pictures

This is not an exclusive list. The e-merchant apply appropriate technical and administrative measures to protect such data. These measures must include appropriate technologies to store, protect and preserve data. Personal data may not be retained except for the purpose of the sales contract and shall not be used for any other purpose without the express prior consent of the consumer. This includes advertising and marketing.

The e-merchant must notify the Ministry of Commerce within three days of learning of any breach. If the consumer and the e-merchant agree on a continuing relationship, then the e-merchant may retain the protected Personal Consumer Data for the purposes of fulfilling transactions pursuant to that relationship. Otherwise, personal information may not be retained.

Only companies formed in accordance with the Saudi Companies Law may register as electronic merchants in the country. E-merchants must comply with all laws and regulations relating to data protection.

CHAPTER TWENTY

Teleworking

The NCA issued Telework Cybersecurity Controls (TCC-1:2021) (TCC) to establish security requirements for working from home. According to the NCA, "the increasing dependence of some entities on telework increases threats and cyber risks to telework systems." These controls are designed to address such risks. The regulation is not limited to the public sector.

The TCC exists in addition to the NCA's Essential Cybersecurity Controls.

The NCA defines teleworking in this context as follows:

> [A]ny technical systems, means or tools and its related components which are used by the organization to enable employees to perform their job duties in a place other than the official workplace. Examples include: virtual meeting systems, collaboration systems, file sharing, virtual private network (VPN), remote access systems, and other systems used in the work environment.

The TCC applies to government agencies and private entities operating critical national infrastructure. It does not apply to private companies that merely process government data. Such companies are nonetheless encouraged to implement the TCC.

The TCC addresses the following subject areas:

* * *

1. Secure use of telework devices and how to protect them.
2. Secure handling of identities and passwords.
3. Protection of the stored data on the telework devices, and to be handled based on its classification.
4. Secure handling of applications and solutions used for telework such as: virtual conferencing and collaboration, and file sharing solutions.
5. Secure handling of home networks, making sure it is configured in a secure way.
6. Avoidance of teleworking using unreliable public devices or networks or while in public places.
7. Unauthorized physical access, loss, theft, and sabotage of technical assets and telework systems.
8. To Communicate directly with the cybersecurity department If a cybersecurity threat is suspected.

Required defense mechanisms include:

1. Managing telework access rights based on need, considering the sensitivi- ty of the systems, the level of access rights and the type of devices used by employees for telework.
2. Restricting remote access for the same user from multiple computers at the same time (Concurrent Logins).
3. Using secure standards to manage identities and passwords used in the telework systems.
4. Applying updates and security patches for telework systems at least once every three months.
5. Reviewing telework systems' configurations and hardening at least once every year.
6. Reviewing and changing default configurations, and ensuring the removal of hard-coded, backdoor and/or default passwords.
7. Securing Session Management which includes the session authenticity, lockout, and timeout.
8. Restricting the activation of the features and services of the telework sys- tems based on needs, provided that potential cyber risks are analyzed in case there is a need to activate

> them.

9.   Restrictions on network services, protocols and ports used to access remotely, specifically to internal systems and to only be opened based on need.
10.   Reviewing firewall rules and configurations, at least once every year.
11.   Protecting against Distributed Denial of Service Attack (DDoS) attacks to limit risks arising from these attacks.
12.   Protecting against Advanced Persistent Threats (APT) at the network layer.
13.   Central management of mobile devices and BYODs using a Mobile De- vice Management system (MDM).
14.   Applying updates and security patches on mobile devices, at least once every month.

Additionally, data sent over a telework network must be encrypted. To avoid ransomware attacks, regular back-ups are required. Classified data sent over the network must be identified and the risk of its use on telework networks identified.

A vulnerability assessment should be performed quarterly, combined with, or including penetration testing. Telework systems must be monitored on a 24/7 basis.

CHAPTER TWENTY-ONE

Data Protection Law

بسم الله الرحمن الرحيم

الرقـم: م/١٩
التاريخ: ٩/٢/١٤٤٣هـ

No 19/M
Date : 09 / 02 / 1443H

With the help of Allah,
    We, Salman bin Abdul Aziz AL Saud
    King of the Kingdom of Saudi Arabia

Based on Article (70) of the Statute of Governance issued by Royal Decree No (91/A) dated 27/8/1412H.

Based on Article (20) of the Cabinet Law, issued by Royal Decree No (13/A) dated 3/3/1414H.

* * *

Based on Article (18) of the Saudi Shura Council Law issued by Royal Decree No (91/A) dated 27/8/1412H.

After perusal of the two resolutions No (19/96) dated 3/7/1442H and No (40/213) dated 3/12/1442H issued by the Saudi Shura Council.

After reviewing the Cabinet Decision No (98) dated 7/2/1443H,

We decided as follows:

First : Approval of the Personal Data Protection Law in its accompanying form.

Second : As an exception to what is stated in Article (43) of the Personal Data Protection Law, the application of what is stated in Paragraph (1) and Paragraph (2) of Article (33) of the Law shall be postponed, as determined by the Head of the Competent Authority and not exceeding (five) years from the effective date of the Law.

Third : The controllers– stipulated in Paragraph (18) of Article (1) of the personal Data Protection Law – shall amend their status in accordance with the provisions of the law within a period not exceeding one year starting from the date of its effective date. The competent authority may – for reasons it deems appropriate- grant additional periods to some authorities to amend their status.

Fourth : The application of the provisions of the Personal Data Protection Law and its implementing regulations does not prejudice the competencies and tasks of the National Cyber Security Authority, as it is a security authority specialized in cyber security and the national reference in its affairs in the Kingdom, in accordance with its organization issued by Royal Decree No (6801) dated 11/02/1439H.

Fifth : His Highness, the Deputy Prime Minister, ministers and heads of independent relevant agencies – each within his jurisdiction – must implement our decree.

Signature : ....

Salman bin Abdul Aziz AL Saud

	In the name of Allah,	
Kingdom of Saudi Arabia	the most gracious, the most merciful	Decision No: (98)
General Secretariat of the Council of Ministers		D a t e d : 7/2/1443H

Cabinet Decisions

The Council of Ministers, after perusal of the transaction received from the Royal Court No. 70420 dated 4/12/1442H containing the Ministry of Interior telegram No. 41168 dated 22/4/1436H regarding the draft of the Personal Data protection Law.

After perusal of the two High Orders No (5727/ب م) dated 23/8/1432H and No. (29549) dated 17/6/1433H.

After reviewing the regulation of the National Cyber Security Authority, issued by Royal Decree No (6801) dated 11/2/1439H.

After reviewing the Law of the Central Bank of Saudi Arabia issued by Royal Decree No (36/M) dated 11/4/1442H.

After reviewing the regulation of the Communications and Information Technology Commission issued by Cabinet Resolution No. (74) dated 5/3/1422H and its amendments.

After reviewing the organizational arrangements of the Saudi Data and Artificial Intelligence Authority issued by Cabinet Resolution No. (292) dated 27/4/1441H.

* * *

After reviewing minutes No (201) dated 1/3/1438H, No. (1135) dated 20/8/1439H, No. (1263) dated 12/7/1440H, No. (215) dated 10/4/1442H, and memos No. (420) dated 25/5/1441H, No. (961) dated 13/6/1442H, No. (1359) dated 15/8/1442H, No. (1783) dated 15/10/1442H, No. (2334) dated 29/12/1442H and No. (73) dated 10/1/1443H prepared at the Cabinet Expert Authority.

After reviewing the minutes of the Council of Political and Security Affairs No. 10664 dated 29/5/1442H.

After reviewing the recommendation No. (D/43/4-1) dated 18/1/1443H prepared by the Council of Economic and Development Affairs.

After considering the two resolutions of the Shura Council No. (19/96) dated 3/7/1442H and No. (40/213) dated 3/12/1442H.

After reviewing the recommendation No. (926) dated 30/1/1443H of the Cabinet General Committee.

Decides as follows:

First: Approval of the Personal Data Protection Law in its accompanying form.

Second: the competent authority shall be the Saudi Data and Artificial Intelligence Authority for two years during which transferring the jurisdiction of supervising the application of the provisions of the law and its implementing regulations to the National Data Management Office – in light of what results from the application of the provisions of the personal Data Protection Law and its executive regulations and in light of the level of maturity in the data sector – shall be considered.

Third: As an exception to what is stated in Article (43) of the Personal Data Protection Law, the application of what is stated in Paragraph (1) and Paragraph (2) of Article (33) of the Law shall be postponed, as determined by the Head of the Competent Authority and not exceeding (five) years from the effective date of the Law.

Fourth: The controllers– stipulated in Paragraph (18) of Article (1) of the personal Data Protection Law – shall amend their status in accordance with the provisions of the law within a period not exceeding one year starting from the date of its effective date. The competent authority may – for reasons it deems appropriate- grant additional periods to some authorities to amend their status.

Fifth: The application of the provisions of the Personal Data Protection Law and its implementing regulations does not prejudice the competencies and tasks of the National Cyber Security Authority, as it is a security authority specialized in cyber security and the national reference in its affairs in the Kingdom, in accordance with its organization issued by Royal Decree No (6801) dated 11/02/1439H.

A draft Royal Decree regarding what is stipulated in clauses (First), (Third), (Fourth) and (Fifth) of this decision has been prepared its form accompanied this one.

Sixth: Coordination shall be made between the competent authority and the Saudi Central Bank to prepare a memo of understanding to regulate certain aspects associated with application of the provisions of the Personal Data Protection Law and implementing regulations at the authorities that are subject to the regulatory supervision of the Central Bank of Saudi Arabia. Determine the role of each of them in this respect, taking into account that the competencies do not overlap between them regarding the application of the provisions of the law and its implementing regulations to the entities subject to the regulatory supervision of the Central Bank of Saudi Arabia, to prevent affecting the independence of the Saudi Central Bank, and the special nature of financial and banking transactions, and in order to enhance the stability and growth of the sectors supervised by the Saudi Central Bank, provided that the preparation of the memorandum is completed and signed in conjunction with the validity of the law.

Seventh: Coordination shall be made between the competent authority and Communications and Information Technology

Commission to prepare memo of understanding to regulate some aspects related to the application of the provisions of the Personal Data Protection Law and implementing regulations to the entities subject to organization of the Communications and Information Technology Commission, and in order to prevent affecting the Communications and Information Technology Commission as an independent organizational authority that supervises sensitive sectors related to personal transactions of individuals, and to enhance the stability and growth of the sectors it supervises, provided that the preparation and signing of the memorandum shall be completed in conjunction with validity of the law.

Eighth: The competent authority shall, in coordinating with authorities it thinks appropriate, carry on continuous awareness campaign for the personal data holders as well as for the employees of controllers – stipulated in Paragraph (18) of Article (1) of the Personal Data Protection Law – or its affiliated employees, to clarify the rights and obligations stipulated in the law after its entry into force.

Ninth: The Controllers – set forth in Paragraph 18 of Article (1) of the Personal Data Protection Law – shall take necessary measures to hold work sessions and the like for their affiliated employees or workers to introduce the vocabulary and principles contained in the law after its entry into force. These authorities shall coordinate with the competent authority whenever necessary in order to provide advice and support.

Tenth: The competent authority, in coordination with the relevant authorities it deems appropriate, to evaluate the results of the implementation of the Personal Data Protection Law and to provide relevant views, including proposing any necessary amendments to it within (five) years from the date of entry into force, and submitting what is necessary to complete necessary actions.

Eleventh: The competent authority, within a period not exceeding (one year) from the date of entry into force of the Personal Data Protection Law, and in coordination with the relevant authorities it deems appropriate, to review the provisions of the relevant laws, decisions and regulations that dealt with provisions related to the protection of personal data for individuals, and to propose amending them in accordance with the provisions of the law, and submitting what requires completion of legal procedures in this regard.

Twelfth: The competent authority, when preparing the implementing regulations of the Personal Data Protection Law, shall take into account the establishment of provisions and controls related to the organizational, administrative and technical procedures and means related to storing personal data with the controllers - set forth in Paragraph 18 of Article (1) of the Law – in a manner that ensures preservation of personal data in accordance with its nature and degree of sensitivity, based on what is stated in Article (19) of the Law.

Signature:_____

Prime Minister

الرقم ـــــــــــــــــــــ

التاريخ / / ١٤هـ

المرفقات ـــــــــــــــــــــ

الـمـملكة العـربية السـعودية

هيئة الخبراء بمجلس الوزراء

Bureau Of Experts At The Council Of Ministers

Personal Data Protection Law

Article (1) :

For the purpose of implementing this law, the following terms and expressions – wherever they are mentioned in this law – shall have the meanings indicated next to each of them, unless the context requires otherwise:

1- **Law** : Personal Data Protection Law.

2- **Regulations** : the Implementing Regulations of the Law.

3- **Competent Authority** : the authority to be determined by a decision of the Council of Ministers.

4- **Personal Data** : Every statement – regardless of its source or form – that leads to the identification of individual specifically or makes it possible to identify him directly or indirectly, including name, personal identification number, addresses, contact numbers, license numbers, records, personal property, bank account numbers, credit cards, fixed or mobile photographs of the individual and other data of a personal nature.

5- **Processing** : Any operation performed on personal data by any means, manual or automated, including collection, recording, preservation, indexing, arrangement, coordination, storage, modification, updating, merging, retrieval, use, disclosure, transmission, publication, sharing of data or interconnection, blocking, erasure and destruction.

6- **Collection** : The controller obtains personal data in accordance with the provisions of the law, whether from its owner directly or from his representative or legal guardian, or from another party.

7- **Destruction**: Every action that leads to remove personal data and makes it impossible to view or restore it.

8- **Disclosure**: Enable any person, except the Controller, to obtain personal data, use it or view it by any means and for any purpose.

9- **Transfer** : Transfer of personal data from one place to another for processing.

10- **Publication** : Broadcasting or making available any personal data through a written, audio, or visual means of publication.

11- **Sensitive Data** : Every personal statement that indicates a reference to an individual's ethnic or tribal origin, religious, intellectual or political belief, or indicates his membership in associations or civil institutions, as well as criminal and security data, biometric identification data, genetic data, credit data or health data, location data and data that indicates that the individual is of unknown parentage or one of them.

12- **Genetic Data** : Every personal statement related to the genetic or acquired characteristics of a natural person that uniquely identifies the physiological or health characteristics of that person, and is extracted from the analysis of a person's biological sample, such as the analysis of nucleic acids or any other sample that leads to the extraction of genetic data.

13- **Health Data** : Every personal statement related to individual's health condition whether physical, mental, psychological condition or related to the individual's respective health services.

14- **Health Services** : Services related to the individual's health including preventive, curative, rehabilitative, hypnotic, and drug provision services.

15- **Credit Data** : Every personal statement related to an individual's request for, or obtaining financing, whether for a personal or family purpose, from an entity that exercises finance, including any statement related to his ability to obtain credit, his ability to meet it, or related to his credit history.

16- **Data Subject** : An individual to whom personal data is related or his representative or legal guardian.

17- **Public Authority** : Any ministry, department, public institution, public authority or any independent public entity in the Kingdom of Saudi Arabia or any of its affiliates.

18- **Controller** : Any public authority and any person of special natural or legal capacity that identifies the purpose of processing personal data, whether the data processing is initiated by it or by the processor.

19- **Processor** : Any public authority and any person of a private natural or legal capacity that processes personal data for the benefit of and on behalf of the Controller.

Article (2)

1- The law shall apply to any processing of personal data related to individuals that takes place in the Kingdom of Saudi Arabia by any means, including processing personal data related to individuals residing in the Kingdom by any means from any party outside the Kingdom, and this includes the data of the deceased if it leads to know him or to specifically know one of his family members.

2- An individual's processing of personal data for purposes not exceeding personal or family use is excluded from the scope of application of the law, as long as he has not published or disclosed it to third parties. The regulations define what is meant by personal and family use as set forth in this paragraph.

* * *

Article (3) :

The provisions and procedures stipulated in the law do not prejudice any provision that grants a right to the data subject or decides to better protect it, provided for by another law or an international agreement to which the Kingdom of Saudi Arabia is a party.

Article (4) :

The data subject, in accordance with the provisions of the law, shall have the following rights:

1- The right to know, which includes informing him of the legal or practical justification for collecting his personal data, and the purpose of that. His data shall not be subsequently processed in a manner inconsistent with the purpose of its collection or in cases other than those stipulated in Article (10) of the Law.

2- The right to access his personal data available with the controller, which includes accessing his personal data and obtaining a copy of it in a clear format identical to the contents of the records, free of charge- as determined by the regulations- without prejudice to the provisions of the Credit Information Law with regard to the material consideration and without prejudice to the provisions of Article (9) of the Law.

3- The right to request the correction, completion or updating of his personal data held by the Controller.

4- The right to request destruction of what is no longer needed of his personal data available with the controller, without prejudice to the provisions of Article (18) of the Law.

5- Other rights provided for by the law indicated by regulations.

Article (5) :

1- Except in the cases provided for by the Law, personal data may not be processed or the purpose of its processing may not be changed without the consent of its owner. The regulations specify the conditions of consent, the circumstances in which the consent must be in writing, and the terms and conditions for obtaining the consent of the legal guardian if the Data subject is incompetent.

2- In all cases , the Data subject, at any time, may refer to the consent indicated in Paragraph (1) of this Article. The regulations shall determine the required controls.

Article (6) :

The processing of personal data shall not be subject to the consent referred to in Paragraph (1) of Article (5) of the Law in the following cases:

1- When the processing achieves a realized interest for the owner of the personal data and the contact with him is impossible or difficult to realize.

2- When the processing is in accordance with another law or in implementation of a previous agreement to which the owner of the personal data is a party.

3- If the controller is a public entity and such processing is required for security purposes or to fulfill judicial requirements.

Article (7) :

The consent referred to in Paragraph (1) of Article (5) of the Law may not be a condition for provision of a service or provision of benefit, unless the service or benefit is related to the processing of personal data for which the consent was issued.

Article (8) :

Subject to the provisions of the law and regulations regarding disclosure of personal data, the controller shall, when choosing a Processor , be committed to select an authority that provides necessary guarantees for the implementation of the provisions of the law and regulations, and controller shall constantly verify the compliance of that entity with the instructions it gives to it in all matters relating to the protection of personal data, in a manner that does not prejudice its responsibilities towards the owner of the personal data or the competent authority, as the case may be. The regulations specify the provisions necessary for this, provided that they include provisions relating to any subsequent contracts made by the Processor .

Article (9) :

1- The controller may determine periods for practicing the right to access to personal data stipulated in Paragraph (2) of Article (4) of the law. The competent authority shall identify the appropriate period. The controller may restrict this right in the following cases:

    a- If this is necessary to protect the Data subject or others from any harm in accordance with the provisions established by the Regulations.

    b- If the controller is a public body and the restriction is required for security purposes, to implement another law or to fulfill judicial requirements.

1- The controller shall not enable the Data subject to access it when any of the conditions stipulated in Paragraphs 1, 2, 3, 4, 5 and 6 of Article (16) of the law are fulfilled.

Article (10) :

The controller may collect personal data only from its owner directly, and such data may also be processed only to achieve the purpose for which it was collected. However, the controller may collect personal data directly from a person other than the owner, or process it for a purpose other than the one for which it was collected, in the following cases:

1- If the Data subject agree to this, in accordance with the provisions of the law.

2- If the personal data is publicly available, or it was collected from a publicly available source.

3- If the controller is a public entity and if collection of personal data from a person other than its owner directly or being processed for a purpose other than the one for which it was collected, is required for security purposes, to implement another law or to fulfill judicial requirements in accordance with the provisions specified by the regulations.

4- If compliance with this prohibition may harm the Data subject or affect his vital interests in accordance with the provisions specified by the regulations.

5- If collection or processing of personal data is necessary to protect public health or safety, or to protect the life or health of a particular individual or individuals. The regulation shall specify the controls and procedures related therewith.

6- If the personal data will not be recorded or stored in a form that makes it possible to identify its owner and know him directly or indirectly. The regulations shall specify the controls and procedures related therewith.

Article (11) :

1- The purpose of collecting personal data must be directly related to the purposes of the controller and shall not conflict with any statutory provision.

2- Methods and means of collecting personal data shall not conflict with any legally established provision, and shall be appropriate to the circumstances of the owner, direct, clear, secure and free of deception, misleading or extortion methods.

3- The content of personal data must be appropriate and limited to the minimum necessary to achieve the purpose of its collection, while avoiding including what leads to know its owner in a specific way when the purpose of collection has been achieved. The regulations shall specify the necessary controls thereto.

4- In the event that it becomes clear that the personal data collected is no longer necessary to achieve the purpose of its collection, the controller shall stop collecting it and immediately destroy what it has previously collected.

Article (12) :

The controller shall adopt a personal data privacy policy and make it available for its owners to view before collecting their data, provided that such policy shall include defining the purpose of data collection, content of the personal data to be collected, method of collection, means of storing data, how it is processed, how to obtain it, the rights of its owner in relation to it and how to exercise these rights.

Article (13) :

The controller shall, in case of collecting personal data directly from its owner, take sufficient means to inform him of the following elements before starting to collect his data:

1- Legal or practical justification for collecting his personal data.
2- The purpose of collecting his personal data, and whether collecting all or some of them is mandatory or optional, and informing him as well that his data will not be processed later in a manner inconsistent with the purpose of collecting it or in cases other than those stipulated in Article (10) of the law.
3- The identity of the person collecting the personal data and his reference address where applicable, unless such collection is for security purposes.
4- Entity or entities to which the personal data will be disclosed and whether the personal data will be transferred, disclosed or processed outside the Kingdom of Saudi Arabia.
5- Potential effects and dangers of not completing the personal data collection procedure.
6- His rights provided for in Article (4) of the law.
7- Other elements determined by the regulations according to

the nature of the activity practiced by the controller.

Article (14) :

The Controller may not process personal data without taking adequate steps to verify its accuracy, completeness, timeliness and relevance to the purpose for which it was collected in accordance with the provisions of the law.

Article (15) :

The Controller may disclose personal data only in the following cases:

1- If the data subject agrees to the disclosure in accordance with the provisions of the law.
2- If personal data has been collected from a publicly available source.
3- If the authority requesting disclosure is a public authority, for security purposes, to implement another law or to fulfill judicial requirement in accordance with the provisions identified by the regulations.
4- If the disclosure is necessary to protect public health or safety, or to protect the life or health of a particular individual or individuals. The regulation shall specify the controls and procedures related therewith.
5- If the disclosure is limited to process the data later on in a way that does not lead to know the identity of the Data subject or any other individual specifically. The regulations shall identify the controls and procedures related therewith.

Article (16) :

The controller shall not disclose the personal data in the cases stipulated in Paragraphs (1), (2) and (5) of Article (15) of the law whenever the disclosure is characterized by any of the following:

1- Poses a threat to security, harms the reputation of the Kingdom or conflicts with the Kingdom's interest.

2- Affects the Kingdom's relations with another country.
3- Prevents detection of a crime, affects the rights of an accused to a fair trial or affects the integrity of existing criminal proceedings.
4- Endanger the safety of an individual or individuals.
5- Entails violating the privacy of an individual other than the Data subject as determined by the regulations.
6- Conflicts with the interest of an incompetent person.
7- Breaches legally established professional obligations.
8- Involves a breach of an obligation, procedure or judgment.
9- Discloses a confidential source of information that the public interest should not disclose.

Article (17) :

1- If an error is corrected, a deficiency is completed or an update is made in the personal data, the controller shall notify any other party to which such data has been transferred, and allow it to make such modification.
2- The regulations shall specify the time periods for correction and updating, the types of correction and procedures required to avoid the consequences of processing incorrect, inaccurate or out-of-date personal data.

Article (18) :

1- The controller shall destroy the personal data as soon as the purpose of its collection ends. However, it may keep such data after the purpose of its collection has ended if everything that leads to specifically knowing the owner of data is removed in accordance with the controls determined by the regulations.
2- The controller shall keep personal data even after the purpose of collecting data is over in the following two cases:

a- If there is a legal justification requiring that the personal data be kept for a specific period, and in this case, the personal data will be destroyed after expiry of such period or the end of the purpose of collecting it, whichever is longer.

b- If the personal data is closely related to a case considered before a judicial body and its retention is required for this purpose. In this case, it shall be destroyed after completing the judicial procedures for the case.

Article (19) :

The controller shall take necessary organizational, administrative and technical measures and means to ensure the preservation of personal data, including when transferred, in accordance with the provisions and controls specified by the regulations.

Article (20) :

1- The controller shall notify the competent authority as soon as it becomes aware of occurrence of leakage or damage to personal data or occurrence of illegal access to it.

2- The regulations shall specify the circumstances in which the controller should notify the Data subject in the event of a leak or damage to his/ her personal data or illegal access to it. If the occurrence of any of the foregoing would cause serious harm to his/ her data or himself/ herself, the controller shall notify him/ her immediately.

Article (21) :

The controller shall respond to the requests of the Data subject regarding his/ her rights provided for in the law within a specific period and through an appropriate means identified by the regulations.

Article (22) :

The controller shall conduct an evaluation of the effects of processing of personal data for any product or service provided to the public according to the nature of the activity practiced by the controller. The regulations shall specify the necessary provisions for this.

Article (23) :

The regulations shall specify additional controls and procedures, in a manner that does not conflict with the provisions of the law, regarding the processing of valid data in a manner that ensures preservation of privacy of its owners and protects their rights stipulated in the law, provided that they include the following:

1- Restricting the right to access health data, including medical files, to fewest possible number of employees or workers and only to the extent necessary to provide the necessary health services.
2- Restricting health data processing procedures and processes to a minimum number of employees and workers to provide health services or provide health insurance programs.

Article (24) :

The regulations shall specify additional controls and procedures, in a manner that does not conflict with the provisions of the law, regarding the processing of credit data in a manner that ensures preservation of privacy of its owners and protects their rights stipulated in the law and in the Credit Information Act, provided that they include the following:

1- Take what is necessary to verify the availability of personal data owner's written consent to collect this data or change the purpose of collecting, disclosing or publishing it in accordance with the provisions of the law and the Credit Information Law.
2- Obligation to notify the Data subject when a request for disclosure of his/ her credit data is received from any authority.

Article (25) :

* * *

With the exception of awareness materials for public entities, the controller may not use personal means of communication, including postal and electronic addresses, of the Data subject to send advertising or awareness materials except in accordance with the following:

1- Obtain the consent of the target recipient to send these materials to him/ her.
2- The sender of materials shall provide a clear mechanism, as determined by the regulations, that enables the target recipient to express his/ her desire to stop sending such materials to him/ her when he/ she wishes to do so.

The regulations shall determine the provisions relating to the advertising and awareness materials indicated in this article, and terms and conditions of the target recipient's consent to sending such materials to him/ her.

Article (26) :

Except sensitive data, the personal data may be processed for marketing purposes if such data has been directly collected from its owner and he/ she agrees in accordance with the law. The regulations shall identify the necessary controls thereto.

Article (27) :

Personal data may be collected or processed for scientific, research or statistical purposes without consent of its owner in the following cases:

1- If personal data does not contain any evidence of the specific identity of its owner.
2- If evidence of the identity of the Data subject will be specifically destroyed during its processing and before it is disclosed to any other party, and such data is not sensitive data.
3- If the collection or processing of personal data for these purposes is required by another law or in implementation

of a previous agreement to which the data owner is a party. The regulations shall identify the necessary controls for what is stated in this article.

Article (28) :

Official documents that identify the Data subject may not be photocopied or copied except when required for implementation of provisions of a law or when a competent public authority requests that such documents be photocopied or copied as determined by the regulations.

Article (29) :

Except in cases of extreme necessity to preserve the life of the data owner outside the Kingdom of Saudi Arabia or his vital interests, or to prevent, examine or treat a disease infection, the controller may not transfer personal data outside the Kingdom or disclose it to a party outside the Kingdom of Saudi Arabia unless for implementation of an obligation under an agreement to which the Kingdom is a party, or to serve the interests of the Kingdom or for other purposes as determined by the regulations, after the following conditions are met:

1- Transfer or disclosure shall not prejudice national security or the vital interests of the Kingdom of Saudi Arabia.
2- Provide sufficient guarantees to maintain confidentiality of personal data that will be transferred or disclosed, so that the standards for protecting personal data shall not be less than the standards contained in the law and regulations.
3- The transfer or disclosure shall be limited to the minimum amount of personal data that is needed.
4- Approval of the competent authority on the transfer or disclosure of data as determined by the regulations.

With the exception of the condition mentioned in Paragraph (1) of this Article, the competent authority may exempt the controller, in each case separately, from complying with one of the aforementioned conditions if the competent authority, alone or jointly with other parties, determine that the personal data will have an acceptable level of protection outside the Kingdom of Saudi Arabia, and that the data is not sensitive data.

Article (30):

1- Without prejudice to the provisions of the law and the powers of the Central Bank of Saudi Arabia in accordance with the provisions of the relevant regulatory texts, the competent authority shall be the authority supervising the application of the provisions of the law and regulations.

2- The controller shall appoint or designate a person (or more) from its employees to be responsible for its commitment to implement the provisions of the law and regulations. The regulations shall determine the provisions related to what is mentioned in this paragraph.

3- The controller shall cooperate with competent authority in order to carry out its tasks related to supervising the application of the law and regulations. The controller shall also take necessary measures regarding the related issues referred to it by the competent authority. The competent authority may request the necessary documents or information from the controller to ensure its compliance with the law and regulations.

4- The competent authority may, at its discretion, delegate other authorities to carry out some of the tasks entrusted to it related to supervising the application of the law and regulations.

Article (31) :

Without prejudice to what is stated in Article (18) of the law, the controller shall keep records for a period specified by the regulations for the activities of personal data processing according to the nature of the activity practiced by the controller, in order to be available when requested by the competent authority, provided that the records include a minimum of the following data:

1- Controller's contact details.
2- Purpose of processing personal data.

3- Description of categories of data subject.
4- Any authority to which personal data has been (or will be) disclosed.
5- Whether personal data has been (or will be) transferred outside the Kingdom of Saudi Arabia or disclosed to a party outside the Kingdom of Saudi Arabia.
6- The expected length of time for retention of personal data.

Article (32) :

1- The competent authority shall establish an electronic portal for the purpose of building a national register of the controllers aiming to monitor and follow up the compliance of these authorities with the provisions of the law and regulations and to provide services related to personal data protection measures for the controllers, as determined by the regulations.

2- All controllers shall register in the Portal referred to in Paragraph (1) of this Article, and the competent authority shall collect a fixed annual fee not exceeding (one hundred thousand) riyals for the registration of controllers with a special legal capacity in the portal referred to in Paragraph (1) of this Article, provided that the regulations shall specify the amount of the fixed annual fee not exceeding the maximum limit determined according to the nature of the activity practiced by those authorities.

3- In the portal, a special record shall be assigned to each controller in which the records referred to in Article (31) of the law and other necessary documents or information related to the processing of personal data shall be recorded.

Article (33) :

1- The competent authority shall be responsible for approving the practice of commercial, professional or non-profit activities related to the protection of personal data in the Kingdom of Saudi Arabia, as determined by the regulations.

2- The authority outside the Kingdom, when processing

personal data related to individuals residing in the Kingdom of Saudi Arabia by any means, shall appoint a representative in the Kingdom to be authorized by the competent authority to carry out its obligations under the law and regulations. Such appointment shall not prejudice the responsibilities of that authority towards the Data subject or the competent authority, as the case may be. The regulations shall identify the provisions related to licensing and the limits of the representative's relationship with the entity he represents outside the Kingdom of Saudi Arabia.

3- The competent authority may license entities that issue accreditation certificates for the controller and the Processor , provided that the competent authority establishes the rules regulating the issuance of such certificates.

Article (34) :

The Data subject may submit to the competent authority any complaint arising from the application of the law and regulations. The regulations shall determine the controls for the competent authority's handling of complaints submitted by the Data subject arising from the application of the law and regulations.

Article (35):

1- Without prejudice to any more severe penalty provided for in another law, the penalty for committing the following violations shall be in accordance with what is written before it:

b- Anyone who discloses or publishes sensitive data in violation of the law: shall be punished with imprisonment for a period not exceeding (two years) and a fine not exceeding (three million) riyals or either of these two penalties if committing such a violation is intended to harm the data owner or to achieve a personal benefit.

c- Whoever violates the provisions of Article (29) of the law: shall be punished by imprisonment for a period not exceeding (one year) and a fine not exceeding (one million) riyals, or by one of these two penalties.

4- The Public Prosecution shall be responsible for the investigation and public prosecution before the competent court for the violations set forth in this article.

5- The competent court shall consider cases arising from the application of this article and impose the prescribed penalties.

6- The competent court may double the penalty of the fine in case of recurrence, even if it results in exceeding its maximum limit, provided that it does not exceed twice this limit.

Article (36) :

1- Any matter in respect of which no special text has been provided in Article (35) of the law, without prejudice to any more severe penalty provided for in another law, every person with a special natural or legal capacity, covered by the provisions of the law, violates any of the provisions of the law or regulations, shall be punished with a warning or a fine not exceeding (five million) riyals. The penalty of the fine may be doubled in the event of repetition of violation, even if it results in exceeding its maximum limit, provided that it does not exceed twice this limit.

2- A committee (or more) with no less than (three) members shall be formed, by a decision of the Head of the Competent Authority. One of the members shall be named chairman and among them shall be a legal or statutory advisor. Such committee shall consider violations and impose the penalty of warning or the fine set forth in paragraph (1) of this Article, according to the type of violation committed, its gravity and the extent of its impact, provided that the committee's decision shall be approved by the head of the competent authority or his authorized representative. The head of the competent authority shall issue, by his decision, the rules of work of the committee in which the remuneration of its members shall be determined.

3- A person against whom a decision has been issued by the committee stipulated in Paragraph (2) of this article has the right to file a grievance against such decision before the competent court.

Article (37) :

1- The employees and workers, named by a decision issued by the head of the competent authority, shall control the violations provided for in the law and regulations.

2- The competent authority shall have the right to seize the means or tools used in committing the violation until a decision is made.

Article (38) :

1- Without prejudice to the rights of third parties in good faith, the competent court may order the confiscation of funds obtained as a result of committing violations set forth in the law.

2- The competent court or the committee provided for in Paragraph (2) of Article (36), as the case may be, may include the judgment or decision issued by either of them determining the penalty stipulating the publication of its summary at the expense of the convict or violator in local newspaper (or more) issued in place of residence or in any other appropriate means, according to the type of violation committed, its severity and the extent of its impact, provided that publication shall be made after the judgment has acquired the final character or the decision has been summarized by the expiration of the deadline for grievance against it, or a final ruling has been issued rejecting the grievance.

Article (39) :

Without prejudice to what is stated in Article (35) and Paragraph (1) of Article (36) of the law, the public authority shall take disciplinary action against any of its employees in the event of violating any of the provisions of the law and regulations, in accordance with the provisions and procedures for accountability and disciplinary procedures established by law.

Article (40) :

Without prejudice to the imposition of penalties provided for in the law, those who have suffered harm as a result of committing any of the violations contained in the law and regulations, shall have the right to claim before the competent court for compensation for material or moral damage in proportion to the extent of the damage.

Article (41) :

Everyone who carries out work of personal data processing shall be obliged to maintain the secrets related to the data even after expiry of his/ her functional or contractual relationship.

Article (42) :

The Head of the competent authority shall issue the regulations within a period not exceeding (one hundred eighty) days from the date of issuance of the law, provided that, prior to its issuance, he shall coordinate with the Ministry of Communications and Information Technology, the Ministry of Foreign Affairs, the Communication and Information Technology Commission, the National Cyber Security Authority, the Saudi Health Council and the Saudi Central Bank.

Article (43) :

The law shall be applied and becomes effective after (one hundred eighty) days from the date of its publication in the Official Gazette.

CHAPTER TWENTY-TWO
PDPL Analysis

PDPL Analysis

There are two documents which enact the PDPL, the Royal Decree formally enacting the legislation, and the Cabinet Decision forwarding the proposed law to the Royal Diwan. Both of these documents contain modifications or suspensions of certain provisions of the original law as originally proposed and so must be analyzed along with the law itself. The Royal Decree gives data controllers (as defined in the law) one year to comply with some of the law's provisions. It also requires the registration of foreign data controllers with SDAIA.

Royal Decree enacting the Personal Data Protection Law

2.   Article 33, ¶¶ 1, 2 are suspended for up to five years as determined by SDAIA. These paragraphs provide that SDAIA "shall be responsible for approving the practice of commercial, professional or non-profit personal data protection activities.

The second paragraph of Article 33 reads:

"The authority outside the Kingdom, when processing personal data by any means related to individuals residing in the Kingdom of Saudi Arabia, shall appoint a representative in the Kingdom to be authorized [by SDAIA] to carry out its obligations under the law and regulations. Such appointment shall not prejudice the responsibilities of the authority towards the Data Subject or the competent authority, as the case may be. The regulations shall identify the provisions related to licensing and the limits of the representative's relationship that he represents outside the Kingdom of Saudi Arabia."

When this section is given effect, it requires foreign data processors to appoint a representative to liaise with SDAIA. That appointment will not affect the relationship among the Data Subject, the foreign processor or SDAIA itself.

3. Data controllers (i.e., those who collect data) have one year to destroy personal data in accordance with Article 18 of the PDPL unless SDAIA grants an extension.

4. Nothing in the PDPL alters the jurisdiction or responsibility of the National Cyber Security Authority.

5. All Saudi agencies must implement this law.

Cabinet Decision No. 98

Cabinet Decision No. 98, dated 7/2/1443 H provides:

Art 2 SDAIA to be the regulator. For two years. {Why? Agency may be renamed or given more or less authority depending on experience during this period.}

Art. 4: Controllers have one year to amend their status in accordance with Article 18. Article 18 deals with destruction of data, not registration of controllers.[103]

Art. 6 SDAIA to coordinate with SAMA and enter into a MOU. Interesting points: "taking into account that the competencies do not overlap between them regarding the application of the provisions of the {PDPL} and the ... "special nature of financial and banking transactions."

Art. 7 SDAIA to enter into an MOU with CITC.

Art. 8, 9: both refer to Controllers and Art. 18(1) of the PDPL. ?

Art. 10 SDAIA to report on the implementation of the law and to provide relevant views with an eye towards necessary amendments.

Art 11 Report within one year   Duplicative?

Art. 12 Provide for data preservation where appropriate.

Personal Data Protection Law

Articles of the PDPL are not given titles. Each Article is titled in this section by section analysis merely for convenience and such titles are not part of the law.

Art 1 Definitions

"Personal data" is that which leads to the identification of an individual.

"Processing" is any operation performed on personal data by any means.

"Sensitive data" is information that leads to "ethnic or tribal origin, religious, intellectual or political belief, or indicates his

---

[103] This appears to be a numbering error in the law.

membership in associations or civil institutions, as well as criminal and security data, biometric identification data, genetic data, credit data or health data, location data and data that indicates that the individual is of unknown parentage or one of them."

In other words,

- ethnic
- tribal
- religion
- other beliefs
- criminal
- security
- biometric
- genetic
- credit
- health
- location
- legitimacy/parentage

Such information is always considered "sensitive" in Saudi Arabia and afforded the highest level of protection.

Article 2 Data Processing

This Article applies to processing of personal data taking place in the Kingdom   including processing taking place outside the Kingdom relating to Data subjects inside the Kingdom.

The deceased are included /deceased have privacy rights in Saudi Arabia.

Article 3 Minimum Standards

The PDPL sets forth minimum standards, if another law provides greater protections, those protections will apply.

Article 4 Right to Know & Correct

Owners (called "Data Subjects") have the right to know what their data is being used for, have the right to a copy of the data at no charge (subject to credit reporting rules) and has a right to correct erroneous data. Owner has the right to request data deletion as well as any other rights provided by law.

Article 5 Consent Required

Consent is required for the processing of data. Some types of consent must be in writing.

Article 6 Exceptions to Consent

Consent not required:

- if the processing is for the owner and contacting him is difficult.
- when the processing is in accordance with another law or in implementation of a previous agreement to which the owner is a party; or
- if the data controller is a public company.

Article 7 Consent not a Condition

Consent may not be a condition of providing the service, unless the service is related to the processing of personal data.

Because most requests for data claim that services will be denied unless data is provided, it would be helpful to know under what conditions this rule will apply. Some examples would be helpful.

Article 8 Selection of Processor

The data controller must select a reliable processor.

Article 9 Period for Holding Data

The data controller may specify the period during which the data is to be held. SDAIA to determine if this period is appropriate.

Right may be restricted to protect others from harm or for security purposes.

Article 10 Owner Collection Only

Personal Information may only be collected from the Owner. Exceptions:

> - Owner agrees
> - Data publicly available
> - Data controller a public entity, for security or to implement another law
> - compliance may harm the Owner
> - necessary to protect public health and safety
> - will not be stored so as to make it possible to identify owner

Article 11 Purpose of Collection

- Data collection must be related to controller's purpose
- Collection methods shall be appropriate
- Info collected must be appropriate
- If no longer needed shall be destroyed

Article 12 Privacy Policy

Controller must adopt a data privacy policy and make it available.

Like the Ministry of labor with its approved work rules, or Ministry of Housing with Uniform Contracts, a template would be helpful.

Article 13 Owner Notification

Prior to collection, the Owner must be notified of the reasons for collection and the need for information along with a summary of Owner's rights.

Article 14 Verification of Information

Controller must verify accuracy, completeness and relevance of data.

Article 15 Permitted Disclosure

No disclosure unless:

- Owner agrees
- data collected from a public source
- for security reasons
- to protect public safety (in accordance with regulatory controls)
- identifying info deleted

Article 16 Prohibited Disclosure

No disclosure at all if:

- threat to security
- diplomatic relations threatened
- impedes law enforcement
- endangers individual safety
- violates third-party privacy
- conflicts with interests of an incompetent/ incapacitated
- breaches professional obligation
- involves a breach of an obligation
- discloses a confidential source

Article 17 Notification of Processor in Case of Correction

If data corrected, transferee must be notified. Regulations will specify time periods for correction and updating and procedures.

Article 18 Data Retention

As soon as data not needed, it shall be destroyed.

May keep data if de-personalized.

Exceptions: data shall be kept where there is:

- legal justification (e.g., taxes); or
- pending judicial case.

Article 19 Preservation of Data

Controller must insure preservation of personal data.

Article 20 Unauthorized Disclosure

SDAIA must be notified in case of leak.

Regulations to specify when Owner to be notified.

Article 21 Requests for Information

Regulations to specify how to respond to Owner requests for information.

Article 22 Study Required

Controller to conduct a study on the effects of data collection on a product or service offered.

Article 23 Additional Controls

Regulations shall specify additional controls and procedures.

Article 24 Credit Reports

Regulations shall cover procedures for credit reports.

Article 25 Prohibition on Advertising

Controller may not send advertising unless:

- with consent
- with easy unsubscribe

This topic to be covered in the regulations.

Article 26 Permitted Marketing

Except for sensitive data, personal data may be used for marketing purposes with consent. Regulations shall cover controls.

Article 27 Scientific

No consent needed for scientific, research or statistical purposes:

- if no specific identity (already identified, why put here?)
- data will be depersonalized during processing
- required by another law

Article 28 Prohibition on Copies

Photocopies may not be made except "when required for implementation of provisions of a law" or when requested by a public authority. Regulations to cover. This will affect due diligence projects and access to court legal files.

Article 29 Prohibition on Transborder Transfer

Data may not be transferred outside Kingdom except:

- cases of extreme necessity
- to prevent or treat infection

unless

- treaty requirement
- to serve the interests of the Kingdom
- as per regulations

only if

- national security not prejudiced
- sufficient guarantees provided
- limited to minimum needed
- Approved by SDAIA as per regulations

SDAIA may make exceptions on a case by case basis where controller provides guarantees.

Article 30 SDAIA Jurisdiction

SDAIA to regulate. Controllers must designate data privacy officer, as per regulations. SDAIA may audit controllers. SDAIA may delegate its powers to other agencies.

Article 31 Records to be Kept by Controller

Controller must keep records:

- contact details
- reason for processing data
- description of data collected
- description of transferees
- whether & to whom data transferred outside KSA
- data retention time

Article 32 National Controller Portal

SDAIA to create national controller portal
All controllers to register in portal, annual fee <100,000 SAR
Article 31 summary included in portal

Article 33 SDAIA Approval Required

- SDAIA to approve personal data protection activities
- Foreign data processor shall appoint in-Kingdom representative.
- Regulations to provide details related to licensing

SDAIA to license controllers and processors

Article 34 Complaints

Owner may file a complaint with SDAIA concerning any matter within itss jurisdiction. Regulations to specify procedures. Not clear if others, such as data controllers, will have similar rights of complaint.

Article 35 Penalties

Unauthorized disclosure or publication: 2 years and up to SAR 3 million if intended to harm Owner or derive personal benefit

Unauthorized foreign transfer: 1 year and up to SR 1 million

Public Prosecution shall investigate and prosecute.

Penalties may be doubled for recidivism.

Article 36 Administrative Penalties

Any violation other than foreign transfer or publication a fine of up to SAR 5 million (no imprisonment). Fine may be doubled in case of recidivism.

SDAIA to set up administrative commitee to consider penalties. Appeals from decisions may be taken to court.

Article 37 Enforcement

SDAIA employees will inspect and record violations of the law

SDAIA may seize equipment used in violation.

Article 38 Forfeiture

SDAIA may seize funds earned through a violation. Final judgments may be published.

Article 39 SDAIA Personnel

SDAIA personnel may be disciplined for violating the law.

Article 40 Private Right of Action

There is established a private right of action in favor of Owners whose data has been disclosed through a violation of the law.[104]

Article 41 Post-Employment Restrictions

Those who work with personal data must maintain confidentiality in perpetuity (after expiration of employment relationship).

Article 42 Implementing Regulations, Required Consultation

Regulations to issue within 180 days of issuance of the law. Coordination with CITC, Ministry of Foreign Affairs, National Cyber Security Authority, the Saudi Health Council and the Saudi Central Bank.

Article 43 Effective Date

Law becomes effective 180 days after publication.[105]

---

[104] There is no requirement that harm or actual damages be established. There is, however, a rule against speculative damages in the Islamic shari'a. So it is not clear how this Article will be interpreted.

[105] The law will take effect on March 23, 2022.

Saudi Arabia Privacy Law

CHAPTER TWENTY-THREE

Acronyms

Acronyms

CITC Commission	Communications and Information Technology
CCRF	Cloud Computing Regulatory Framework
DAMA	Data Management International Association
EU	European Union
FOIR	Freedom of Information Regulations (Saudi Arabia)
FTC	Federal Trade Commission (USA)
GDPR	General Data Protection Regulation (European Union)
NCA	National Cybersecurity Authority (Saudi Arabia)
NDMO	National Data Management Office
ODIR	Open Data Interim Regulations (Saudi Arabia)
PII	Personal Identifiable Information
PDPL	Personal Data Protection Law (Saudi Arabia)
PDIR	Personal Data Protection Interim Regulations

* * *

SAIP Saudi Authority for Intellectual Property

SAMA Saudi Arabia Monetary Authority

SDAIA Saudi Data and Artificial Intelligence Authority (Saudi Arabia)

SSOT Single Source of Truth (KSA Data Originator)

WTO World Trade Organization

About the Author

Michael O'Kane is an attorney with fifteen years' experience in Saudi Arabia and the Middle East. He is a former special legal advisor to the Kingdom of Saudi Arabia and in that capacity drafted a legal code, including a disputes resolution code, for the Kingdom's Economic Cities project. He advised the Saudi Railways Commission and assisted them in drafting national regulations. He advised KA-CARE, the King Abdullah City for Atomic and Renewable Energy in drafting a law for the peaceful use of nuclear energy in the Kingdom. His book, *Doing Business in Saudi Arabia* is on Amazon's International Law bestseller list. He is the author is *Doing Business in Saudi Arabia, Saudi Securities Law, Saudi Labor Law Outline; Saudi Real Estate Law, Law and Rockets: An American Lawyer in Iraq* and *Saudi Arabia Export Guide.* He is rumored to be the author of *Don't Forget to Tape the Toilets: The Missing Employee Orientation Manual for Saudi Arabia and Bahrain.*

He may be contacted at mok@mu7ami.com.